SCM RESEARCH

Undoing Theology

Undoing Theology

Life Stories from Non-normative Christians

Chris Greenough

This edition published in the UK in 2018 by SCM Press
Editorial office
3rd Floor, Invicta House,
108–114 Golden Lane,
London EC1Y 0TG, UK

SCM Press is an imprint of Hymns Ancient & Modern Ltd
(a registered charity)

13A Hellesdon Park Road, Norwich,
Norfolk NR6 5DR, UK

www.scmpress.co.uk

British Library Cataloguing in Publication data

A catalogue record for this book is available
from the British Library

978 0 334 05621 8

Printed and bound in Great Britain by
4edge Ltd

Contents

To Mark Edward, my first teacher of queer theory

Acknowledgements

This book would not exist but for the efforts and commitment of its three protagonists: Alyce, Caddyman and Cath. I thank each of them for their time and for sharing such intimate life experiences with me. I am humbled by their generosity and I hope I have done justice to each of their stories.

This book is largely the product of my PhD thesis. I offer endless thanks to the most patient, emotionally intuitive, reliable, efficient and knowledgeable supervisor, Dr Deryn Guest. It is a privilege to work with you; I thank you not just for your insightful feedback to my endless drafts, but for your cheery encouragement throughout and your continued support.

In addition to my colleagues, I would also like to express my gratitude to the following academics. To the talented Prof. Helen Newall at Edge Hill University, who designed the cover image for the book. To Dr Hannah Bacon, for our creative and illuminous email exchange on the Tranity in Chapter 3; and to Dr Robin Bauer for his comments on Chapter 5. I also thank Dr Karen Wenell for her feedback on two chapters. Thanks to Prof. Andrew Yip for his thorough (!) and engaging examination of my PhD thesis, his enthusiasm for my work and for his post-award advice. Also, to Prof. Ben Pink Dandelion who served as internal examiner.

I thank the team at SCM Press for their commitment to the publication of this book. To David Shervington, who saw the potential in the publication from our initial communication and to Mary Matthews, editorial manager. Special thanks go to Lawrence Osborn, for his diligent work on the manuscript.

Any errors or mistaken notions within this book are, of course, my own.

Personally, I thank my dad and my brothers (Frank, Bernie and

Neil), sister (Tricia) and auntie Ann for their loyal support. I'm also grateful to my close friends who happily listened to my musings over the course of this work, especially to Becky Fiddler, Helen Thomas, Marie Bennett and Monika Reece. During the time of studying for my PhD, my beloved mother died unexpectedly. I am not sure if she would have approved of the contents of this book, but I know she would have been proud of my achievement!

And finally, to Mark, my partner and soul mate. I cannot thank you enough for your belief, wisdom, insight and support. You taught me to be brave.

Introduction

My favourite game as a young child was church. Of course, child's play is an attempt at recreating and exploring adult contexts, which is why children reconstruct imaginary scenarios by playing house, school and hospital scenes. They attempt to repeat what they observe adults do. Mostly I played church at home with my brothers, who often participated, somewhat reluctantly, as they attempted to consume as many of the white chocolate buttons I used as the Eucharist. I did not know it was an unusual game until my requests at primary school, where I speculated on serving a much bigger congregation, were rebuffed and mocked. I still have the prayer book that I used to preside over my living room religious ceremonies; it sits within my bedside cabinet.

Stimulating my creative play was my insistence on attending as many of the Catholic Masses my mum would obligingly take me to at weekends in our local church. I knew how to say every response, and did so boastfully, but I did not understand most of them. Until the age of about 11, I attended church weekly and served as an altar boy for a brief stint, until my clumsy disposition resulted in numerous accidents (including, setting fire to my cassock and dropping the consecrated Holy Communion). Aside from church, I liked to play house, but my preference was to be the mum and arrange all the tea sets out nicely. Again, this was unpopular with my friends, who were mainly boys. Retrospectively, I see what a queer child I was.

Impassioned by my liberal religious studies teacher, I loved my lessons in school. I remember one particular bath time experience when I received my call to priesthood at the age of 14 during a period of my life where I was wrestling with the dawn of the new consciousness of my hidden homosexuality. The priesthood, in my teenage wisdom, would be an ideal haven to avoid marrying a woman. Aware of the disadvantage of leading a celibate life as my body was rife with hormones, I quickly dismissed my calling, convincing myself it was dizziness from the steam in the bath, which was hardly likely as, in a household of seven, bathwater was recycled two or three times.

These earlier experiences have served to fuel this book which explores the life stories of non-normative Christians. The above account of my youth draws on my own experiences which I choose as personally and theologically relevant to my undertaking of this project. Yet I am unable to reconstruct the past and provide a narrative that is true to the actual events with any confidence. Nonetheless, these memories form part of my youthful religious consciousness and serve as an early marker of my own non-normative development.

Non-normative Christians

Queer theory has become, rapidly, a major discourse within the academy. No discipline within arts or sciences has been unaffected, pioneering much-needed research exploring minority sexualities and non-normative practices. Within theology and religious studies, queer theologies have encouraged us to see God, the Bible and religious practices differently and queer theory has informed explorations of religion from a sexual perspective. Yet, despite this much-needed pioneering academic work, the biographies of sexual migrants are significantly under-researched. There exist only few texts detailing religious experience-based work founded in lesbian, gay, bisexual stories.[1]

Queer research seeks to undermine categories of identity and my use of the term 'queer' incorporates all non-normative lives, which are not necessarily understood in terms of identities. Diana Fuss's essay 'Inside/Out' encourages us to 'to erode and reorganize the conceptual grounds of identity' (1991, p. 1). Therefore, although lesbian, gay, bisexual, transgendered, intersex lives fall neatly into an oft-used acronym LGBTI, I am in agreement with Daniel Warner, who states, 'queer research should stop adding letters to LGBT research, and should instead form a body of knowledge about how these categories come to be, and are lived, on a daily basis' (2004, p. 335).

> At the bottom line of queer theologies, there are biographies of sexual migrants, testimonies of real lives in rebellions made of love, pleasure and suffering. (Althaus-Reid, 2003a, p. 8)

This statement from Marcella Althaus-Reid, appealing for real-life stories in theology, provides the catalyst for my work. Accordingly, my use of the term non-normative is inclusive, as it extends to all 'sexual migrants', referred to by Althaus-Reid, and whose self-identifications or sexual practices counter traditional Christian teaching and positional statements on sexuality.

Gayle Rubin termed those who migrate because of their sexuality 'sexual migrants':

> Many sexual migrants have been thrown out by their families, and many others are fleeing from the threat of institutionalization. Any random collection of homosexuals, sex workers, or miscellaneous perverts can provide heart-stopping stories of rejection and mistreatment by horrified families. (1993, p. 22)

This term is used by Althaus-Reid (2003a, p. 8) but without explicit reference to Rubin. Given the often unsupportive, hostile environments and the negativity of religious pronouncements towards those who practise non-normative sexualities, the term is appropriate.

The purpose of this book is to explore the content of the spiritual and religious journeys of three protagonists Alyce, Caddyman and Cath, with the aim of engaging with personal, experiential theologies. In this, I am concerned with the cumulative impact of traditional theological discourse regarding sexuality on the lives of my participants in relation to their Christian allegiances. Moreover, I explore how previously held belief systems are renegotiated as personal theologies change.

As this book is based upon experience as a source for theology, my principal claim is that storytelling needs to play a more pivotal role in grounding sexual theology. I pay attention to how non-normative praxis connect with Christianity, yet my approach is more inclusive as I explore a diverse range of non-normative sexual practices, including the queerness of 'straight' sexual practice. Indeed, to work solely within the parameters of queer theology would reinforce a binary between straight theology, which would remain unmarked, and queer theory, which is significantly marked. Sexual stories in theology offer a new landscape shaped largely by work in the field of queer studies, but theology must become more inclusive to expose and explore all non-normative, non-vanilla sexual migrants. This results in life stories that add colour and diversity to theology.

Tracing the development of sexual theology from James Nelson, through to Althaus-Reid, Chapter 1 explores the importance of life stories as a source for theology. The chapter examines the transformative potential of sharing sexual stories, and engages with wider sociological, religious and theological engagements with sex and sexuality. Chapter 2 is split into two parts. In Part One, I explore the act of sexual storytelling in addressing a lacuna within practical theology, largely by building on the work of Ruard Ganzevoort. The critical appraisal and fusion of the literature reveals how sharing stories is important for theology because it is relational and it helps people make sense of their lives. Such work has a lot to contribute to practical theology, and I engage with practical theology by attending to the lives of those who have traditionally felt uncomfortable in Christianity due to their non-normative identities. Within Part Two, I discuss the queer enterprise of disturbing and disrupting. In this context, I use queer theory to 'undo' the theoretical framework which allows queer investigators to disrupt and abandon traditional theological approaches. This allows for creative, reflective and intuitive outcomes to emerge from the storytelling.

Exploring non-normative life stories from an experiential perspective led to in-depth online interviews with the three protagonists of this book. There is content within these pages of a sexually explicit nature. Each narrative chapter contains the words offered by each participant, and they have consented to their full usage in this book. Confidentiality and anonymity is especially important for non-normative participants and Christians, as there is a real threat of religious or prejudice-based violence and possible fear of reprisals if respondents are recognized. Therefore, all participants have used a pseudonym to protect their identities, and equally any details which could potentially identify a participant have been obscured. Despite my efforts to ensure anonymity, participants are free to self-disclose aspects of their life in other contexts, which may occur in the public domain. In Chapter 3, I present my first participant, an intersex-identifying Catholic, who self-identifies as made in the image of God. In Chapter 4, I uncover the emotional involvement of researching life stories by interacting with a former 'ex-gay' religious leader, who preached conversion therapy to gay and lesbian Christians, but who ultimately accepted his own homosexuality and acknowledges the detrimental effects of such 'therapy'. Chapter 5 reveals my third protagonist, who identifies as a Christian and engages with bondage practice as a form of prayer that brings her closer to God. Each of the narrative chapters within the book offers space to each of the protagonists without attempting to make their stories blend or overlap in any way.

Throughout these narratives, the role of experience is prioritized as a source for theology. Yet queer theory is built on disruption. Lisa Isherwood asserted that 'Marcella believed that theology had to be built on earthquakes and that its job was not to heal the ruptures that such seismic shifts create but rather engage with and encourage the discontinuity' (2010, p. xvi).

Continuing the mission of discontinuity, in Chapter 6 I discuss how experience itself needs to be 'undone' too. Indeed, I argue that what is required of all theology is to be 'undone'. Finally, I consider the role of disruption and the rupture of repetition as part of queer theology and other theological troublemaking.

1

Life Stories and Sexual Theology

The platform for exploring life stories of non-normative individuals sits between two fields of theological enquiry: sexual theology and practical theology. The primary aim of this chapter is to place my work alongside the relevant fields of study with reference to sexual theology. Accordingly, this chapter is split into two thematic sections. The first section traces the emergence of sexual theology, from its inception with James Nelson, to the radical theological praxis of Marcella Althaus-Reid. The chapter then considers the transformative potential of sexual storytelling and explores the sociological investigations of Andrew Yip. What becomes apparent is that theology about sex and sexuality emerging from Nelson is developed within feminist theology, and later queer theology. Indeed, in academic terms, feminist and queer theory has provided space for discourse on sexualities. Therefore, commentators such as Elizabeth Stuart, Robert Goss, Lisa Isherwood and Susannah Cornwall, among others, aid the discussion of sexual theology and its development into the realm of queer theology. Their scholarship is pertinent to my exploration of the lives of sexual migrants in the production of an inclusive sexual theology. The work of these contributors characterizes an approach that exposes just how sexual contemporary Christian lives are, not just in relation to minority sexualities or practices, but across the sexual continuum. Furthermore, I expose how queerness infects the whole discipline of theology, as a generic category, rather than being a designated subcategory of queer theology. The sexual stories provide more than a contribution to queer theology; they are part of a process by which theology is being revealed as having always been sexual.

Seeking Sexual Theology: James Nelson

Significant non-religious work on sexual practice which pre-dates Nelson's theology includes the two studies by Kinsey and Shire Hite. Although Nelson does not cite these works, they form an important backdrop to theoretical investigations of sexual practice. Kinsey's two key publications (Kinsey et al., 1948, 1953) dealt with *Sexual Behaviour in the Human Male* and *Sexual Behaviour in the Human Female* respectively. Within these texts, Kinsey put the notion of the sexual continuum firmly on the map. In his introduction to the scale, he states:

> Males do not represent two discrete populations, heterosexual and homosexual. The world is not to be divided into sheep and goats. It is a fundamental of taxonomy that nature rarely deals with discrete categories ... The living world is a continuum in each and every one of its aspects (Kinsey et al., 1948, p. 639).

The Hite Report on female sexuality was first published in 1976. It described the sexual practices and fantasies of 100,000 women aged 14 to 78. Information gathered from real-life interviews are reported within the book, which include non-normative practices.

James Nelson is a significant precursor to the work of Althaus-Reid, as he was the first theologian to use the term 'sexual theology' and his book *Embodiment* (1979) provides the basis of his manifesto. Nelson explores sexual diversity under the chapter heading, 'sexual variations', where he is at pains to specify his preference for the term 'variations' rather than 'deviations', as a more positive lexicon. Among the variations Nelson explores are fantasy, masturbation, oral-genital practices, anal intercourse, sadomasochism and porn-ography (1979, p. 158). Equally inclusive of the variations, Nelson also encompasses the 'sexual disenfranchised' in his theology of embodiment, including 'the physically disabled, the seriously ill, aging and mentally retarded [sic]' (1979, p. 211). Linda Woodhead credits Nelson as a lead thinker in arguing that 'the Christian doctrine of the incarnation of God in Christ should reorient sexual reflection by reminding us of the value and importance of the human body' (1997, p. 102).

Nelson's term 'sexual' becomes synonymous with 'incarnational', 'embodiment' and 'body' throughout his work. He justifies the importance of his term, by relating it to the new emerging trends in theology in the 1970s, as a term similar to 'black theology' and 'liberation theology' (1979, p. 15). His use of the term 'sexual' extends beyond a simplistic notion of acts involving genitalia: 'sexual theology is body theology ... our bodies-as-selves give shape to the way in which we feel about the world and about others' (1979, p. 20). Nelson does not offer clear reasons for collapsing the sexual self into the embodied self. Yet, something is lost by not acknowledging this distinction, as the sexual or erotic becomes diluted in favour of a more generalized and broader framework. Certainly, 'embodiment' is less of an explosive topic than 'sex'. Nevertheless, to maintain focus on the inception of sexual theology, we note how for Nelson this emerging discussion of sexuality, in theological terms, locates sexuality as embodied, and, in turn, relational. Nelson's theology issues an important mandate to the Christian churches, calling on them to recognize the church as a sexual community. Such relational ethics underpin Nelson's theology of embodiment in articulating how a community is a part of the development of self. It is this acceptance of self as a sexual being which enables the acceptance of others and theologically, this is the foundation of communion – with others, and with God. Of course, this is not simply a case of add sex to theology and stir, as Nelson explains:

> Resexualizing our theology does not mean putting sexuality into a theology from which it has always been absent. It has always been there. It means a new level of consciousness about the ways in which our sexuality, for good and for ill, has shaped our expressions of faith. (1979, p. 236)

For Nelson, the interface of human sexuality and theology is a two-directional affair, where both sexual theology and the theology of sexuality set off from different starting blocks. His first method involves viewing the embodiment of sexuality as a basis for theology, and this he terms sexual theology. The second approach is to use a traditional approach (the Bible, the Christian

9

tradition and other sources of faith) in exploring what such sources say about sexuality, thereby providing theologies of sexuality. Isolating one of these methods would result in a unidirectional and hierarchical approach to theology, while engaging in both results in a dialogical approach which Nelson favours. However, I argue that this dialogical approach becomes an insurmountable hurdle, which results in a non-explicit methodology.

In Lisa Cahill's review of *Embodiment*, she states that 'Nelson does not explicitly develop a fundamental methodology for Christian ethics' (1979, p. 491). Her major critique is one I share: that Nelson fails to provide a methodology that allows Christians to incorporate sexuality (especially sexual minorities) into the communal life of the church's ministry. Nelson's contribution does not develop a fluid methodology, and by seeking to function two-directionally rather than 'bottom up', he is therefore unable to provide firm foundations for a grounded, embodied, communal theology based on embracing human sexuality. It is among the work of theologians who have built on Nelson's courageous thinking, such as Althaus-Reid, that a methodology of storytelling is offered as one approach, yet Althaus-Reid's offer of such a methodology is equally underdeveloped as I note later on in this chapter. Situating my argument among the work from Nelson and Althaus-Reid in valuing the importance of sexual theology, I offer an approach that uses ethnographic research paradigms, but which is grounded in a queer approach to sexual storytelling, which is detailed in Chapter 2.

My final explanation for how my approach to sexual theology differs from Nelson's is one that results from acknowledging his time of publication. Developments in feminist and queer theory and in the understanding of gender and sexuality since the publication of his work mean that Nelson's writing is limited by binary terminology. To cite one simple example: 'sexuality is our self-understanding and way of being in the world as male and female' (1979, pp. 17–18). This cannot be seen, however as a critique of his work, but an expression indicative of the period of his publication. It is within the new climate of queer studies that Althaus-Reid's work on sexual theology began to appear.

Being Sexually Conscious: Marcella Althaus-Reid

Following Nelson, Althaus-Reid reframed this notion of all theology as sexual by using examples of *Indecent Theology*, in her book of the same title (2000a). She scandalized by encouraging theologians to remove their underwear to write theology, engaging sexuality and sensuality consciously rather than unconsciously when reading, writing and engaging with theology. Her challenge to theologians is to be sexually conscious, whether one's sexuality is considered non-normative or not. Her invitation to think theologically while going commando is extended to straight theologians too.

Kwok Pui-Lan ponders on how traditional Christian doctrines would look if we use Althaus-Reid's lens, as she reminds us of the inclusive nature of sexual theology:

> Sexual theology is not just the specific concern of queer, gay, lesbian, bisexual and transgendered theologians – as it is often assumed to be – but a project that all theologians, whether consciously or unconsciously, participate in. (2003, p. 151)

Althaus-Reid's knicker-less, indecent theology compels theologians to remember that Christian theology is itself

> always and foremost, a Sexual Theology. Based on sexual categories and heterosexual binary systems, obsessed with sexual behaviour and orders, every theological discourse is implicitly a sexual discourse, a decent one, an accepted one. (2000a, p. 22)

Althaus-Reid establishes how the conventional way of engaging with systematic theology has always been inherently sexual and this has always been repressed. However, the kind of sexual theology envisaged by Althaus-Reid is cognizant.

The term *heteronormative* was coined by Michael Warner in the early queer text *Fear of a Queer Planet* (1991), which builds on the concept of 'compulsory heterosexuality' developed by Adrienne Rich in her work of the same title (1980). Compulsory heterosexuality refers to the way society compels participation within heterosexuality as a form of social organization (Waites,

2005). Therefore, Althaus-Reid seeks to undo the heteronormative assumption within Christian theological discourse. Until the advent of feminist and queer scholarship, heteronormativity in theology production has remained unquestioned, so much so that it has largely gone unnoticed, just as questions of race and class have equally and largely been overlooked. Althaus-Reid seeks to make visible this heteronormative assumption.

The transformative power of work already conducted in the area of religious studies of sexuality cannot be underestimated (for example, Stuart, 1997a; Goss, 1998; Yip, 2000; 2002; 2003a; 2003b). Indeed, the political activism with church groups established around LGBTI identities has put the question of sexuality at the forefront of theological and ecclesial debates in the major Western churches. In fact, nowadays, the inclusivity of the church is often brought into question through discussions of sexual morality. That said, my work moves beyond sexual identities and holds a greater focus on the subjectivity of lives and sexual practices which are considered non-normative.

The Injunction for Sexual Stories in Theology

For Althaus-Reid, there is a personalized narrative framework at the basis of queer theology, where we find 'biographies of sexual migrants, testimonies of real lives in rebellions made of love, pleasure and suffering' (2003a, p. 8). She describes the process of telling sexual stories as acts of 'oral sex' (2000a, p. 134–35). Sexual stories rooted in real lives derive from individual self-reflection and offer a platform to theologize from our own experiences. She thus calls for sexual life stories as a valid context for producing individual, personal theological reflection, based on life experiences. Graham Ward observes how sexual theologies have been sanitized by traditional doctrines promoting heterosexual ideals:

Christians do not have a good record when it comes to developing sexuate theologies. In the past they have sanitized their holy desire, purging it of libidinal excesses, fearful of such excesses; or they have read certain socially endorsed heterosexual ideologies into their doctrines of God. (2010, p. 174)

The call for biographies of sexual migrants is therefore a necessary injunction, but Althaus-Reid follows Nelson in failing to provide a methodological overview of how these theologies should be produced. Aside from very brief snippets – such as the example of Argentinian lemon vendors, which is discussed below – the in-depth, subjective, sexual stories Althaus-Reid calls for are lacking in her own work and have not been adequately addressed in academic terms by other theologians. It is precisely the lacuna this book seeks to fill.

Althaus-Reid's call for sexual theology is one which expands beyond queer theology: it is a call for all theology. She demonstrates how the generic category of theology is always sexual, but this sexual potency is rendered impotent because it is hidden. Her 'indecent theology' is an exposé of what was previously repressed, as she calls to light stories that have been previously marginalized, secreted, buried. For Althaus-Reid, the need for sexual stories in theology is essential to disturb, disrupt, challenge and undo what she describes as 'T-theology' (Totalitarian theology; 2003a, p. 8), which is largely the product of white, heterosexual males. Susannah Cornwall states that T-theology is 'Althaus-Reid's shorthand for Western systematic theology which apotheosizes its own historical out-working, not acknowledging its shifting, unfolding quality or its dubious alliances with capital imperialism' (2010b, p. 95).

Indeed, T-theology is a vanilla theology; a myth of decency which is challenged by the theologians who remove their underwear and begin theologizing from the basis of their own real experiences. T-theology is decent theology, which seems to have become the dominant, legitimate form of currency for religion.

The Story of Althaus-Reid: 'A Complex Compañera'

With a continued focus on life-story research, it is important to provide a biographical overview of Althaus-Reid, as ascertained through her own work, as well as within the work of some of her academic contemporaries, critiques and collaborators. I move beyond the work produced by Althaus-Reid as a pioneer of queer theology and now seek to focus on her life story.

> It was in the city of Rosario, Argentina in the 1960s, as part of the liturgy of confession and first communion that I knelt down in what was part of a normative thing to do for Catholics. ... Boys were expected to kneel in front of the priest, who used to sit on a low chair for the purposes of children's confession. Girls were expected to kneel also, but at the right side of the priest ... As I recall it now, insecure about what I was expected to do, I decided to follow what my (male) cousins did and instead of kneeling at the right side of the priest's chair I assumed the position straight opposite the priest's genitalia. I refused to move from there. (Althaus-Reid, 2003a, p. 10)

Althaus-Reid's early childhood memory of being reprimanded for her incorrect positioning during her first communion is one which she reviews with a retrospective critical lens exposing how gender and sexuality relate to the church's structure. This is one of two memories of her youth which are recorded in her work. A second account takes place during her teenage years, when she provides an account of when she and her mother and were evicted:

> I was an adolescent when my family faced eviction. We were given 24 hours to pay overdue rents or leave our house. When the police arrived my mother and myself moved out our few belongings on to the street: some bags of clothes, a box with tea and rice, two chairs. The neighbourhood stood still as if in mourning for yet another eviction; another family put out in the street with a few suitcases and couple of chairs. (2004a, p. 74)

Body and feminist theologian, Lisa Isherwood, coedited a number of texts with Althaus-Reid (2004; 2007a; 2007b; 2008). Isherwood (2010) describes Althaus-Reid as a 'dear friend' (2010, p. xv). Her introduction to *Dancing Theology in Fetish Boots: Essays in Honour of Marcella Althaus-Reid* (2010) provides some brief personal details on Althaus-Reid, describing her as:

A very complex theologian, a Quaker who carried more than one rosary on her person at all times and, when in London, often visited the British Museum to offer a gift to Bast, the cat goddess of the night; and also regularly attended the Church of Scotland. (2010, p. xv)

Although Isherwood's introduction is brief, other authors in the volume expand and locate Althaus-Reid's personal history through their own acquaintances and relationships with her. Althaus-Reid was born in Rosario and moved to Buenos Aires, as Mary E. Hunt describes:

She was a student at Instituto Superior Evangélico de Estudios Teológicos (ISEDET), the ecumenical Protestant faculty in Buenos Aires, where she earned her first degree with an eye toward ministry in the Methodist Church of Argentina. (2010, p. 18)

She subsequently moved to Scotland to establish literacy projects in some of the poorer areas, which led to a doctorate in the University of St Andrews in 1993. Althaus-Reid was also active in the Metropolitan Community Church in Argentina and Scotland.

Starting her academic career, Althaus-Reid's PhD was entitled *Paul Ricoeur and the Methodology of the Theology of Liberation*. Ricoeur's influence on meaning/event and language/experience are detailed within her thesis, and are closely linked to her call for location of author and reader in producing contextual theology. Following her doctorate, she secured a lectureship at Edinburgh University where she became a senior lecturer, reader and professor. She was the first female to hold a professorship in theology at the university (Herald Scotland, 2009).

Althaus-Reid's theology is formulated and communicated from a Latin American based liberation background. Mary E. Hunt claims that 'Marcella was both Latina and global at her core' (2010, p. 18). In agreement, Ivan Petrella states that 'Marcella was a unique voice not just within Latin American liberation theology, but within contemporary theology as a whole … [Her work] wasn't restricted to Latin America or read only by Latin Americans' (2010,

p. 200). However, in the same volume, eminent feminist theologian Rosemary Radford Ruether describes her puzzlement at the fact that Althaus-Reid was well known in the global West, but relatively unknown in Latin America. She states:

> I wrote several inquiries to Latin American feminist theologians and was told that no one had read her and that she wrote in English and wasn't really seen as a Latin American thinker. (2010, p. 254)

She continues, 'I protested that her major book, *Indecent Theology,* was in Spanish and that everything she wrote constantly referenced her Argentinian context' (2010, p. 254). This begs the question as to whether Althaus-Reid's work was perhaps too controversial for the Latin American context. From this I deduce that her reception in the English-speaking world was largely a result of the fact she had completed her PhD in Scotland and was academically active within this context, basing her theoretical work on contemporary European philosophers. Moreover, perhaps she chose not to remain in a country that had seen her evicted onto the streets, instead finding a more liberal environment in Scotland. That said, it is undisputed that Althaus-Reid's work contains innumerable references to her Latin American roots. She, herself, makes reference to her position in the global West and having reached what she terms 'calm waters' within the academy and her relationship with religious authorities (2004a, p. 2), but then is faced with the challenge of how her position could be seen as a betrayal to the poor in her own continent:

> The fact is that few accusations could be more hurtful to any intellectual such as myself, born and bred in Latin America, than betraying the cause of the poor. But women doing theology are always accused of betrayals. (2004a, pp. 2–3)

This seems to be quite a confessional moment of self-positioning, fully aware of her current professional standing as a highly regarded and prestigiously placed academic within the global West, yet arguably removed from the people whom she advocates in her theological writings: the poor, the oppressed, the other. It is not insignificant that the biographical story of her eviction through poverty noted above appears within the same text following her discussion of betrayal.

Althaus-Reid herself describes the type of theologian who is indecent and queer:

> An Indecent theologian is a theologian who has learnt to survive with several passports. She is a Christian and a Queer theologian or a minister and a Queer lover who cannot be shown in public and she is a woman and a worker: the list of the game of multiple representations extends. A Queer theologian has many passports because she is a theologian in diaspora, that is, a theologian who explores at the crossroads of Christianity issues of self-identity and the identity of her community, which are related to sexuality, race, culture, and poverty. (2003a, p. 7)

Robert Shore-Goss attributed Althaus-Reid's own description of a queer, indecent theologian as an autobiographical description, although, he acknowledges, 'she would humbly dismiss that possibility' (2010, p. 2). In preparation for a discussion about the challenges of Althaus-Reid's work, the opening lines of Elizabeth Stuart's contribution to *Dancing Theology in Fetish Boots* (2010) sum up the influence of her personality on her work:

> Marcella Althaus-Reid reminded me of the Holy Spirit. She was fiery, sometimes incomprehensible, blowing into a room whether in person or through her texts overturning and uprooting all that came within her path. You never quite knew where she was going next. She was full of life, of love, and of passion. She shocked, she scandalized, she delighted. (2010, p. 113)

Radical Theological Praxis

> Radical theological praxis always starts with the living experiences of people who do radical things in their lives. (Althaus-Reid, 2001a, p. 60)

Althaus-Reid's contribution to Christian theology was radically indecent and sexualized. This section details some of her major theological concepts, including the knicker-less lemon vendors, her critique of Mariology, the use of bisexuality as a theological method, non-normative concepts of God - all of which challenged the boundaries of Christian thought.

My journey through Althaus-Reid's theology is accompanied by critiques from contextual theologians, such as Kwok Pui-Lan, Mary E. Hunt, Jeremy Carrette and Angela Pears. Then I consider the future-proofing of sexual theology following the loss of Althaus-Reid.

Althaus-Reid's first published book, *Indecent Theology* (2000a) was described by Kwok Pui-Lan as 'wild and courageous' (2003, p. 156). The book opens with the call for theologians to produce a theology without underwear, which she relates to the removal of underwear by lemon vendors on the streets in Argentina:

> The lemon vendor sitting in the street may be able to feel her sex; her musky smell may be confused with her basket of lemons, in a metaphor that brings together sexuality and economics. But the Argentinian theologian may be different. She may keep her underwear on at the moment of prayer. (2000a, p. 1)

Mayra Rivera Rivera describes this as 'one of the most startling (and memorable) opening scenes in contemporary theological texts' (2010, p. 79). Mary E. Hunt commends Althaus-Reid on lifting the skirts of these lemon vendors, before lifting the skirts on God, which came later in Althaus-Reid's theological thought (Althaus-Reid 2004a). Hunt continues 'it never occurred to me to think about what was beneath their skirts. Marcella imagined it, analysed it, and wrote about it' (2010, p. 18). Such a provocative sexual and erotic style had hardly been imagined before in the production of Christian theology. The description of the lemon vendors resonated with her readers who grasped its potential to denude other areas of discourse. Lisa Isherwood, for example, immediately sees the need for feminist theology to confront its own sexual lacunae. In her response to *Indecent Theology*, Isherwood notes how Althaus-Reid makes the leap from traditional feminist theological writing to sexual theological writing:

Marcella, thank you, you have presented a tantalizing challenge to feminist theology, you have asked us all to face the vulva and get over the womb. You are quite right when you assert that many of us have been prissy in the face of pleasure, sex and explicit language! (2003, p. 141)

The vendors also provided a starting point for Althaus-Reid's critique of Mariology. Isherwood comments that she 'distrusted Mariology but had medals of Mary and saints around her neck' (2010, p. xv). In Chapter 2 of *From Feminist to Indecent Theology* Althaus-Reid positions Mary as 'a rich white woman who does not walk' (2004a, p. 30). She is suspicious of Mary's virginity, and her elevated status means poor woman cannot identify with her. Her critique of Mary is that Mary does not dwell among us and is devoid of any sexualization; women such as the Argentinian lemon vendors cannot identify with her:

We should work out if there is a María among us, in the face of our sisters, a María who is a street vendor, a child in the slums, a battered woman and a chica cleaning the room of a rich lady. Perhaps only then will God the white upper-class woman become God among us women in Latin America. (2004a, p. 43)

In critiquing Mary in such a way, Althaus-Reid was also aware of her own betrayal of poor women, as she portrays in her description of leaving Argentina for Scotland and pursuing a career in academia, noted in her confessional above.

Althaus-Reid described herself as a bisexual theologian. I am unsure if she identified as bisexual in terms of sexual orientation, but it is clear from her work that she used critical theological bisexuality as an attempt to challenge the heteronormative matrix of Christianity. The 'Bi/Christ' allows theologians to imagine 'the reality of people's identity outside heterosexualism [and] binary boundaries' (2000a, p. 117), and, following Ricoeur, it 'gives us something to think about' (2000a, p. 118). In *The Queer God* (2003a), Althaus-Reid quantifies the positionality of bisexuality as important to theology:

What we are trying to say here is that independently of the sexual identity of the theologian as an individual, theology is the art of a critical bisexual action and reflection on God and humanity. The interesting thing about this is the bisexual critical epistemology could be considered one of the main challenges for any theologian. (2003a, p. 15)

The pronoun usage of 'we' in this quotation rubs against a later claim from Althaus-Reid and Isherwood that 'Queer theology is an 'I' theology. The theologian doesn't hide in a grammatical essentialism, for instance, to use a 'we' which presumes the authority of an academic body' (2004, p. 6). I presume that the preference of personal pronouns in queer theological writing had not quite been worked out in the publication of *The Queer God* in 2003.

A Bi/Christ refuses to be caught up in heteronormative assumptions, and it is through visioning this capacity for intimate relations across the gender spectrum that our thinking is challenged. Christ's bisexuality is not a historical Christological fact or a call for further investigation, but simply suggesting that Christ is bisexual provides a platform by which he can be reimagined and liberated from the heteronormative constraints in which he has historically been framed by T-theology. In other words, it is an ethical and queer imperative to allow individuals to articulate who Jesus is for them, and not restrict the sexual identity of Jesus to narrowly assumed heterosexuality. Kwok Pui-Lan comments that theologizing bisexually 'we might be less prone to thinking in a heterosexual dyad, which has dominated the theological tradition for so long' (2010, p. 40). Bisexual theologies are therefore not a sexual orientation, but a theological stance.

Yet, Mary E. Hunt remains unconvinced that bisexuality from a theoretical perspective actually serves to challenge the binary matrix:

I am not persuaded that bisexuality challenges binary categories. To the contrary, it seems to reinforce the heterosexual-homosexual split precisely in claiming – thus re-inscribing – both. (2010, p. 23)

Although Hunt's contestation of bisexuality as a stance for queer theologizing is all too brief, I am inclined to agree. Althaus-Reid's image of a Bi/Christ as a tool for theological reflection is a significant one, as it does remove Christ from the constraints of heterosexuality in which he has been framed. But the development of her notion of a theologian who adopts bisexuality as a heuristic tool, rather than an ontological identity, does reinforce the binary matrix.

The sexually orientated, self-identified bisexual theologian Margaret Robinson comments that 'Althaus-Reid's critical bisexual theology is a method and not an identity', and that she has 'concerns about it being co-opted by non-bisexuals, to our detriment' (2010, p. 110). Robinson also notes that Althaus-Reid confuses bisexuality with polyamory. It is important to remember that one can be bisexual and monogamous or celibate. It may have been more helpful to adopt a heuristic tool such as polyamory, or pansexuality to envisage an inclusive Christ, although Althaus-Reid may interpret Christ's bisexuality as an open and fluid approach to intimate relations with others.

It was not only Christ who Althaus-Reid sought to liberate from the shackles of compulsory heterosexuality. Her project for liberation theology seeks to liberate the poor, oppressed and sexually exotic as well as God. Althaus-Reid interrupts the Christian tradition of envisaging God with a heterocentric and patriarchal lens, which has resulted in, for many outsiders and sexual migrants, an inhospitable God. *The Queer God* (2003a) she envisages is one rediscovered outside of heterosexual ideology and a God who is marginal, standing among the deviant and the damned. The Queer God is a stranger God, one who walks with the poor and the queer.

Reimagining God outside the framework of heteronormativity has been labelled as heretic and blasphemous. In one example, Rolland McCleary's blog post (2009) is an example of a critic who judged her work as blasphemous. The blog, entitled 'Marcella Althaus-Reid: Theology's Bisexual Shock Jock and Queen of Obscene' is well informed and contains details of her life and work. The lengthy post concludes (in my opinion, harshly): 'There's no accounting for tastes or beliefs, but we should recognize doctrines of theo-porn guru, Marcella Althaus-Reid, were very wrong. Marcella suggested we might need to be forgiven for loving God (2003a, p. 1). I suggest people need to be forgiven for loving Marcella in her role of blasphemer.' For Althaus-Reid, theology as a sexual act, she acknowledges, 'takes obscenities to orthodoxy and orthopraxy' (2000a, p. 87) and she is aware of the critical reception of her work. She reflects:

> Writing *Indecent Theology* was part of a theological journey that was conflictual but also cathartic and healing for me ... My problem was that I did not want to publish my manuscript. I wrote it for me and my friends and it was good for us ... All sorts of fears haunted me ..., such as losing friends, curtailing my theological professional status and killing my mother with a heart attack just when she thought I was finally settled into life and normalcy. (2003b, pp. 182–3)

Indecent Theology encourages the use of language that disrupts and challenges the traditional style in which theology has been written. Kwok Pui-Lan states that the use of such language

> subverts the traditional decent rhetoric of theology and may indeed be labelled as "perverse" in some conservative circles. Since sex has the dimension of fun, risk and transgression, sexual theology pays attention to expressions and performances that subvert the status quo (2003, p. 151).

I follow Koosed's phrasing of this: 'I experience a perverse pleasure, gaiety if you will, in writing in ways a biblical scholar is not supposed to write' (2006, p. 343).

A number of voices reference the disruption and controversy caused by Althaus-Reid's scholarship. Jeremy Carrette comments how you read Althaus-Reid's work 'with either disgust or delight (perhaps always both)' (2001, p. 289). He describes her style of writing as 'flirtatious' and her 'sensual delights' as 'indulgent' (2001, p. 288). Acknowledging, however, that the aim of Althaus-Reid's work is to do more than 'to shock, scandalise and titillate' (2001, p. 289), he considers her work 'a serious intellectual project to "mutually imbricate" ... different domains of knowledge' (2001, p.

289). Like Carrette, Pui-Lan sees Althaus-Reid's use of language as 'shocking' and that the shock is testimony to 'the degree which we have been indoctrinated by the patriarchal and heterosexual myth-making of the Church' (2003, p. 155). There is a playfulness, a parody in Althaus-Reid's use of these terms, and her aim is a 'sexual ideological disruption within Christianity' (2003, p. 9). Angela Pears elicits and develops the tactic shock used within Althaus-Reid's opus:

> This juxtapositioning of the theological and the sexual in such pairings is part of her strategy of confrontation. It uses language in such a way as to invite shock and then for the reader to begin to unpack why the use of language in this way has this impact. (2004, p. 147)

Dancing Theology in Fetish Boots (2010) is a collection of essays in tribute to Althaus-Reid, both honouring and critiquing her contribution to theology following her death. In one chapter, Hunt comments that Althaus-Reid was 'unconcerned for career or personal gain' (2010, p. 25) and this engendered a bravery in her approach to theology. Yet, 'there were perhaps contradictions in the person and work of Marcella Althaus-Reid' (Sands, 2010, p. 44). Hunt comments, 'Marcella laughed to think that her readers thought she was involved in all of the sexual practices she described and permitted' (2010, p. 25). In aligning the production of queer sexual theology to a form of art, Hunt relates her work to the genre of surrealism, as she comments:

> Like the work of other artists of the surreal, Marcella's many essays and books, edited collections and lectures are full of surprises, twists and turns, the unexpected, strange pairings. Her work encompasses odd and, at times, random thoughts. (2010, p. 17)

Tina Beattie exercises a similar critique in her review of *From Feminist Theology to Indecent Theology*, as she considers the anticipated audience of Althaus-Reid's work:

It is hard to see who this kind of language is directed at. It is far too convoluted to appeal to a general readership, and it is far too sloppy and unfocused to appeal to an academic readership. At the very least, one might wish that the publisher had employed a more ruthless copy-editor to tidy up the almost impenetrable prose. (2007, p. 470)

She concludes that the work is 'anti-Christian diatribe, and a poorly written one at that' (2007, p. 471). Continuing with the theme of her writing style, Hunt states:

Reading her work is not an easy task. Challenges jump off every page. Some ideas don't make a lot of sense on first reading, and some don't make any more sense even on second or third reading! Images and references vary so widely as to give the impression that one is on a theological rollercoaster with no end to the ride in sight. (2010, p. 21)

Unfortunately, Althaus-Reid's untimely death in 2009 did signal an end to the pleasures of her theological ride. Hunt is concerned with the gap her death has left in theology, 'I am saddened by her premature end and troubled by the fact that there is no obvious replacement in the wings' (2010, p. 17) and 'as I have mourned her loss I realize it is made worse by the fact that we are too few queer theologians to begin with. There is not another Marcella in the pipeline, as far as I know' (2010, p. 30).

It is undisputable that Althaus-Reid's contribution to queer theology is a significant one. She has led the way for others to follow by highlighting the creativity needed to pave out new theological pathways and possibilities for non-normative identifying individuals, who have been obscured by traditional heteronormative theology. Sex, built on passionate and playful foreplay, an intuitive negotiation of bodies, can be an intense, pleasurable experience. On the contrary though, at times, it can be all too brief, somewhat of an anti-climax. In such terms, I am amused by Grace Jantzen's statement:

But I have found myself wondering, 'And then what?' Like a child who knows there must be more to a story, I have turned round in my mind how this account of Christendom and queer living might continue. (2001, p. 276)

Elizabeth Stuart reiterates this post-sex comedown by posing the post-coital question 'is that it?':

> The whole point about sex is that is offers only temporary satisfaction. This is why we tend to want to do it more than once. But also at its best and most satisfying it offers the promise of something beyond itself, of an ecstasy that does not fade, or a connection that does not return to the shallows. (2010, p. 114)

In continuing and honouring Althaus-Reid's legacy, theologians ensure that indecent sexual theology is imaginative, valid, powerful and intelligently credible enough to continue to challenge the normative assumptions of theology. Aside from challenging mainstream normative theologies which have denied the existence of non-vanilla sexual practices and perversions, sex in theology can be fun, intimate, satisfying, fantastical and a release. Moreover, sexual stories are a potent catalyst for transformation.

The Transformative Potential of Sexual Stories

The call for sexual stories has been echoed by several other theologians and sociologists. Joseph Gelfer, in his book on masculine spiritualities *Numen, Old Men,* states that '"sexual storytelling" is an important part of queer theology' (2009, p. 147). Robert Shore-Goss's chapter 'Dis/Grace-full Incarnation and the Dis/Grace-full Church' (2010) reiterates Althaus-Reid's injunction to mobilize sexual storytelling as a theological framework. Shore-Goss reminds us that queer theology disrupts mainstream theology, which denies or elides the lives of sexual migrants. He reiterates Althaus-Reid's invitation to sexual storytelling as a catalyst for theology, as her 'epistemology of sexual stories of the poor and the sexual outcast disrupts the idealistic and decent boundaries of decent theology' (2010, p. 8).

With reference to emerging trends which highlight the

transformative potential of sexual stories, there are five emergent subthemes which I now go on to explore: (i) stories are transformative because they are relational; (ii) stories can help individuals make sense of their lives; (iii) stories are messy; (iv) stories disrupt the binary between material and divine; (v) stories have the potential to mark and queer heterosexuality.

(i) Stories Are Transformative Because They Are Relational

Storytelling is not done in isolation. Although the act of writing and documenting one's story can be a reflective, solitary task, it is the sharing of stories which brings individuals into relationality with one another. Equally stories are non-neutral; they are charged with subjectivity and individualist interpretations; some are masked by ego. Yet stories evoke emotions in the recipients.

Ken Plummer's seminal text *Telling Sexual Stories* refers to sexual storytelling as a 'sociology of stories' (1995, p. 6). His position that sexual stories are 'joint actions' is one that I agree with. There are 'sexual story tellers who write the lengthy autobiographies' (1995, p. 20) and 'closely allied to these tellers are a second kind of producer: *the coaxers, coachers and coercers. ...* They probe, interview, and interrogate' (1995, p. 21). The third major group are 'the *consumers, readers, audiences* of sexual stories' [his emphasis] (1995, p. 21). Although Plummer uses quite intrusive verbs such as 'probe' and 'interrogate' to describe the role of the collector of such stories, as a 'coaxer, coacher and coercer', I would prefer to adopt the following, less penetrative verbs to describe my actions as researcher in relation to the tellers of sexual stories: *elicit, extrapolate, encourage.* Aside from 'reader', the terms Plummer uses for his third major group *consumer* and *audience* have sexual points of reference. For example, the term 'consumer' has connotations of active destruction or exploitation. The term 'audience' sets out the reader as voyeuristic, an onlooker. Without shying away from such sexual terms, I am happy with his term 'reader' as it offers no presuppositions.

Sexual stories can be categorized as 'coming out' stories, as individuals share stories that reflect individual desires, fantasies, relationships and sexual practices. Plummer uses coming out stories from a homosexual perspective to demonstrate how they are applicable to all lives:

> It tells initially of a frustrated, thwarted and stigmatised desire for someone of one's own sex – of a love that dare not speak its name; it stumbles around childhood longing and youthful secrets; it interrogates itself, seeking 'causes' and 'histories' that might bring 'motives' and 'memories' into focus; it finds a crisis, a turning point, an epiphany; and then it enters a new world – a new identity, born again, metamorphosis, coming out. (1995, p. 52)

Indeed, the language used to structure such stories is significant. Andrew Yip places value on a non-academic storytelling approach which complements social scientific methodologies:

> Accompanying the development of social scientific literature is the emergence of anecdotal narratives and personal biographies … The importance of such writings cannot be denied. They often offer moving and powerful stories of courage, resilience, and wisdom. In many ways, they could be more effective than scholarly writings precisely because they are not wrapped in academic language. (2010a, p. 48)

As Nelson envisaged the transformative potential of the church as a sexual community, Plummer, writing from a secular perspective, believes that 'intimate citizenship' makes a difference (1995, p. 16). This notion of intimate citizenship can be re-evaluated in religious terms. Paul Heelas and Linda Woodhead discuss a 'subjective turn' (2005, p. 2) in which individualization trumps institutionalism and notions of self are valued more highly than institutions such as churches.

To further explore social interpretations of subjective sexual identities, Gayle Rubin has conceived a hierarchal structure of sexual practices, which form a sexual pyramid. She states:

> Marital, reproductive heterosexuals are alone at the top of the

erotic pyramid. Clamouring below are unmarried monogamous heterosexuals in couples, followed by most other heterosexuals. Solitary sex floats ambiguously ... Stable, long-term lesbian and gay male couples are verging on respectability, but bar dykes and promiscuous gay men are hovering just above the groups at the very bottom of the pyramid. The most despised sexual castes currently include transsexuals, transvestites, fetishists, sadomasochists, sex workers such as prostitutes and porn models, and the lowliest of all, those whose eroticism transgresses generational boundaries. (1984, p. 279)

Althaus-Reid states that it is the sexual stories from the bottom of the erotic pyramid that have the most 'transformative potential' for theology (2000a, p. 146). The transformative potential for individuals in constructing religious sexual testimonies is a form of theological political activism. Seeking sexual stories may provide a pathway to bring about change in the institutional forms of religion - religion which has taught many to be ashamed of themselves.

(ii) Stories Can Help Individuals Make Sense of Their Lives

People tell sexual stories to assemble a sense of self and identity. (Plummer, 1995, p. 172)

One of Ken Plummer's rationales for sharing sexual stories is that they are both life-enhancing and a tool for self-development. Similarly, Leanne Tigert reminds us of the importance of telling such stories: 'like Scripture, the stories of our lives enrich us and one another with the telling' (1999, p. 77). Plummer observes how 'history, memory and nostalgia' allow an individual to create 'a sense of the past which helps to provide continuity and order of the flux of the present' (1995, p. 40). Similarly, Bessel Van der Kolk states that 'human being are meaning-making creatures. As they develop, they organise their world according to a personal theory of reality' (1996, p. 304). Indeed, ethnographical studies of narrative research within social sciences remind us that experiential narrative interviews are not a neat form of research, as storytelling is very rarely neat.

Here, I am discussing the non-uniform structure of telling the story, in the next section I discuss the 'messy' content of life stories. Therefore, personal and subjective interpretations are sometimes regarded as problematic as they comprise a 'reconstructive element' (Kohli, 1981, p. 67). Norman Denzin's pioneering work in the field of narrative inquiry and autoethnography takes a sociological approach to conducting empirical research, and he points out that all research is interpretative and constructed anyway (2004, p. 484). All narration is one-sided and individual, and while memories are very personal, Steph Lawler informs us that narratives are 'organized through culturally shared, socially situated and temporal resources' (2002, p. 252).

Since its development within psychotherapy in the 1980s, narrative therapy holds that people can make sense of their lives by structuring their own life events. Peter Reason and Peter Hawkins state that such storytelling enables an individual to make sense of their own contextual experience by narrating it in oral or written form, forming a 'methodology of meaning-making as part of human inquiry' (1988, pp. 81–2). Thus it follows that forming one's life experience as a narrative helps an individual to externalize their feelings and re-author their lives through the deconstruction of their own story.

One example of this is Leanne Tigert's *Coming Out Through Fire* (1999), which shows the transformative power of speaking out about one's own experience. Tigert's work reveals experiential homophobia in the lives of LGBT individuals, and what she terms the 'trauma' of homophobia. She advocates giving a voice to such trauma in order to communicate past hurt, begin transformation and share understanding. There are benefits to the individuals who choose to share their sexual stories within theological frameworks. Tigert states:

Speaking the truth in one's life to heal the past and change the future is a sacred call of the present ... there is the experience of speaking as confrontation, that is, telling your story to those who have been part of your oppression, explicitly or implicitly. (1999, p. 52)

This idea of using narrative as a healing process is one adopted by therapists and counsellors who have worked with religious and faith issues among lesbian, gay, bisexual and transgendered individuals. In *Pink Therapy* (1996) Bernard Lynch's chapter notes that exploring one's own stories seeks to reconcile the spirit within. Thus, narrative therapy 'can explore positive aspects, redefine negatives ones and develop an affirming model of the spirit' (1996, p. 204). In a similar vein, Michael Kocet, Samuel Sanabria and Michael Smith (2012) promote a four-part framework for counsellors to enable them to recognize the importance of resolution between sexual and spiritual conflicts among LGBT religious people. The first part of this framework values the importance of religious and spiritual beliefs in the lives of non-normative individuals. Secondly, the therapy looks at unresolved feelings within the client, using narrative as a means to explore these issues. Thirdly, the therapy aims to enable the client to reconcile sexual and spiritual identities, and finally the client is encouraged to find a connection within the community.

Sharing sexual stories can aid one's self-understanding. Sexual stories provide a catalyst for transformation from self-hate to self-love for individuals who have been shamed by their sexual selves, as they have been regulated by Christian discourse which is obsessed with policing sex. It enables individuals to move from sexual shame to embracing themselves.

Therefore, the use of storytelling can help individuals make sense of their lives, reconcile past events and foster an empowering sense of self. James Pennebaker and Janel Seagal summarize the benefits to individuals of engagement with narrative methodologies:

> The act of constructing stories is a natural human process that helps individuals to understand their experiences and themselves ... Constructing stories facilitates a sense of resolution, which results in less rumination and eventually allows disturbing experiences to subside gradually from conscious thought. (1999, p. 1243)

(iii) Stories Are Messy

> Doing theology on the basis of our experience is not easy, it will
> often be painful, messy and dangerous. (Stuart, 1997a, p. 27)

Elizabeth Stuart, a pioneer of gay and lesbian theology, advocates
learning to trust our own experience. She is right in asserting
that using experience as a starting point for theologizing takes
risk. Mobilizing such experience-based narratives as a source of
theological enquiry is indeed a 'messy' undertaking. For example,
Rachel Mann's autobiography describes her journey through chronic
illness, disability, transitioning gender and her faith. Mann makes a
point about theologizing from the basis of life stories, which echoes
Stuart's assertion, stating 'trying to produce a theology through the
prism of life rather than in the realms of pure ideas will always be
messy' (2012, p. 14).

Sexual storytelling is particularly messy because of multiplicities;
sex lives are complex. In theological terms, the structure and
order of the divine and of religion have often stood apart from
the complexities and messiness of actual lives. Jeremy Carrette
warns that 'the question is how embodied and how messy theology
can become before it will lose control of its utterances' (2001, p.
291). In this, he refers to the undermining of grand narratives
within theology as queer theology seeks to subvert. His call for a
preservation of the master narratives within theology is one that
is at odds with indecent and queer theology. Yet his concern must
be recognized in the lives of Christians who seek stability in their
religion, because their lives are so messy.

Stephen Pattison's observation on pastoral theology working
alongside the attributes of wisdom, intuition and mystery as part of
self-transformation is helpful here. He embraces the messiness of
life juxtaposed against stable religion as a space for transformation.
He labels this transformative potential as 'soft knowledge' yet its
value to personhood and theology is immeasurable. Pattison notes:

> The point about transformational knowledge is not just that
> it is messy, and in a sense amounts to informal knowledge,
> personal knowledge and that elusive thing, 'wisdom' ... It is also

knowledge which arises to a large extent from people's experience of living. It is knowledge directed towards actually changing or transforming people. (2007, p. 206)

Equally reluctant to make neat the messiness of daily lives is Susannah Cornwall. She differs from Pattison as she explicitly brings God into the mess. That said, she does not offer an explicit explanation of how an encounter with the divine can occur or be transformational:

> Messiness in the tradition should not be cleaned-up, sanitized or bowdlerized, for to do so is to make neat and safe what is recalcitrant and profoundly risky and to limit the spheres appropriate for human encounter with the divine. (2010a, p. 225)

(iv) Stories that Subvert the Material/Divine Binary

It is not a question of seeking space within traditional theology to accommodate the stories of messy lives. Queer theology itself must provide a liminal space where the messiness of life and the sanctity of religion can coexist. At this point, the human encounter with the divine is transformational and transformed. Althaus-Reid's sexual theology reveals a false distinction between the materialistic and divine concepts embodied within theological discourses, as she adopts Madonna's popular song to state 'we are all material theologians living in a material world' (2003b, p. 183). In subverting the grand narratives of Christianity, Althaus-Reid's theology is founded firmly in the messiness of life, seeking to challenge traditional understandings of Christianity.

Her distinction is one in which the theological realism of experiential lives is pitted against theological idealism of tradition. Shore-Goss highlights the potential in exploring such stories to challenge the false constructions of the material and the divine within theology:

> Queer sexual theologies are different from idealistic processes because they start from people's sexual action and [Marcella]

notes that sexual theology is doing theology from their own experiences and sexual stories. Such a contextual queer location reveals the falsity of constructions between the material and the divine dimension of human lives. (2010, p. 8)

Thus, from a queer perspective, the binary of personhood and divinity is erased. This relegation and devaluation of grand narratives seeks to embrace a theology that is inclusive. Such inclusivity welcomes the experiences of all non-normative sexual migrants.

(v) Stories that Mark and Queer Heterosexuality

The stories of sexual migrants may therefore help to formulate theologies that reconceptualize God, Christ and the dominant heterosexual frameworks within which theology has traditionally been crafted. Theologians writing from their heterosexual frameworks without the self-awareness of how this positionality informs their theology can often lead to blind heterosexism in theology. Sexual storytelling should never be exclusive to non-heterosexuals. Indeed, queer heterosexuals challenge dominant theological ideologies by stretching the border and playing with the socially privileged starting point of heterosexuality. Althaus-Reid states 'let us remember here that the Genderfucker may also be straight' (2003a, p. 68) and similarly, Joseph Gelfer reminds us that 'straight voices have always been a part of the queer chorus' (2009, p. 114). Gelfer cites Eve Kosofsky Sedgwick as one of those voices, noting that 'there has been a tendency for these straight voices to be female … straight men have been less inclined to question notions of normativity and sexual identity, enjoying as they do its privileges' (2009, p. 114).

Queer heterosexuality is a relatively new phenomenon as a theoretical model, and it explores how normative assumptions and ideals located within heterosexuality have also regulated, confined and imposed limitations on straight-identifying individuals (see, e.g. Wittig, 1992; Thomas, 2000). Althaus-Reid invites heterosexual-identifying individuals to participate:

The theological method of sharing sexual stories requires that everybody engage with honesty in a theology which takes distance from sexual ideologies. It requires that heterosexuals come out of their own closets too, in order to discuss issues such as monogamy, fidelity and family structures, because they are crucial for Christian theology and practice. (2004b, p. 105)

In terms of previous ethnographical studies of non-normative Christians, sociologist Andrew Yip has extensively explored the religious beliefs of non-heterosexual Christians using empirically based research and his findings have been widely published (1997a; 1997b; 1998; 2000; 2002; 2003a; 2003b; 2005; 2010b). The next section moves the discussion into a sociological framework in order to consider how Yip's work on non-heterosexuals can be fruitfully aligned with the theology of Althaus-Reid, in order to continue the disruption of sexual theology to include all non-normative sexualities.

Sociology, Sexuality and Religion: Andrew Yip

Yip's doctoral study examined the life stories of gay male Christian couples, where he explored themes such as: how gay couples meet, how they share life together, how conflict is managed within the relationship, financial arrangements, sex, faith and gay subcultures (1997a). Following this study on gay male Christians, Yip completed a further major work on sexuality (2002; 2003a; 2003b), in which he conducted and analysed the data collected from 565 gay, lesbian and bisexual Christians who completed a 17-page postal questionnaire about their faith and attitudes towards Christianity, and then interviewed a subsample of 61 respondents. His research looked at the persistence of faith among non-heterosexuals (2002), the beliefs of non-heterosexual Christians (2003a) and the relationships between non-heterosexuals and the church (2003b). Yip accessed his respondents through publicity leaflets which were distributed through various channels: through non-heterosexual groups/organizations whose members are exclusively or predominantly Christian (e.g. the Lesbian and Gay Christian Movement); 'secular' gay rights groups/organizations whose members might be Christian (e.g. Stonewall, the legal reform group); Christian groups/organizations whose members might be non-heterosexual (e.g. Centre for Creation Spirituality); the non-heterosexual 'scene' (e.g. pubs, clubs, restaurants); personal contact networks; and snowballing through first level respondents.

During the interviews he used quantitative research methodologies, including asking participants to rate, in order of importance, four elements Yip considered central to Christian faith: personal experiences, the Bible, human reason and church authority. His research overall demonstrates that individualism prevails over institutionalism, with personal experiences and human reason triumphing over the foundations of authority posed by the churches and the Bible. Yip notes, 'individuals are increasingly empowered to actively construct their religious faith, rather than uncritically relying on views prescribed by authority structures' (2002, p. 201). His research covered a large section of those involved in mainstream denominations – Church of England (48 per cent), Roman Catholic (26.4 per cent), Methodist (29.5 per cent) (Yip, 2003a, p. 141) – and his work triangulated both quantitative and qualitative methods.

Many of Yip's published journal articles detail the quantitative data results published from his research findings, but his earlier text, disseminating his thesis (1997a), details a more qualitative approach to his fieldwork through the narratives of the lives of his 68 participants. The major themes of his study include cohabitation, domestic life, desire for same-sex blessings, power relations, personal values and managing stigma as gay Christians.

Yip (2010a) outlines key ideas emerging in sociological, political, theological and queer discourse. He observes how theologians have sought to 'turn theology upside down' (2010a, p. 40) as he comments:

> Their explicit aim is to develop a sexual theology and ethics that adopts a 'bottom up' approach; one that prioritises embodiment and experience, rather than 'top-down' systematic theology that dichotomises the body and the spirit. This is a theology that is not afraid of the body, its desires, wants and passions. (2010a, p. 40)

This chimes with Althaus-Reid's call for theologies from the bottom of the sexual pyramid developed by Rubin, discussed earlier.

Yip's own sexual story can be found in the introduction to his book *Gay Male Christian Couples* (1997a) in which he narrates his coming out story as a gay man through the lens of his sister's response in 1994. Yip had informed his sister that he was in partnership with a man, she had only met once called Noel (1997a, p. 1). In her letter to Yip, she admits to her previously distorted view of gays, 'like their being "sissy", or perhaps being sick or abnormal' (1997a, p. 2) but her view changes when gay sexuality becomes no longer abstract but part of the identity of her close sibling. Her reply to Yip is heart-warming and worth quoting in full:

> In any case, I want to tell you that I fully accept you as you are. You are my brother, a very dear human to me and I love you: gay or not gay. You and your friends, gay or not gay, are always welcome to my home … The important point is I hope you are happy now. (Yip's sister, 1997a, p. 2)

As Althaus-Reid was calling for alternative stories from sexual dissidents from a theological background, Yip was underway conducting extensive fieldwork to seek life stories from gay males. It is staggering to note that despite their heavy contribution to non-normative theology which emerged in tandem in sociological and theological arenas, Althaus-Reid makes no reference to Yip in any of her published texts, and Yip only makes bracketed reference to Althaus-Reid noting her contribution to theology from a non-European context (2005, p. 60). This could be a result of academic boundaries and differences, because of their distinct disciplines: sociology and theology.

In light of the above discussion, it is clear that the trajectory of sexual theology and queer theology contain many cross-fertilizing elements to consider. The sharing of sexual stories makes an important contribution to the fields of theology and sexuality. Therefore, responding to Althaus-Reid's injunction for sexual stories and viewing Yip's research as a useful forebear to my work, attention now turns to the contribution sexual stories can make in terms practical theology.

2

Perverting Practical Theology

I use the term 'pervert' as a shorthand for all the stigmatized sexual orientations. It used to cover male and female homosexuality as well but as these become less disreputable, the term has increasingly referred to the other 'deviations'. Terms such as 'pervert' and 'deviant' have, in general use, a connotation of disapproval, disgust, and dislike. I am using these terms in a denotative fashion, and do not intend them to convey any disapproval on my part. (Rubin, 1984, p. 36)

Practical theology needs perverting. By perverting, I borrow Althaus-Reid's notion of 'per/versions', meaning that alternative interpretations and points of view exist aside from the dominant hegemony (2004b, p. 107). Although Althaus-Reid described her work as contextual, liberational, queer and indecent, she never claimed to be a practical theologian. Yet Riet Bons-Storm describes her work in such terms:

[Althaus-Reid's] point of departure is the understanding that every theology implies a conscious or unconscious sexual and political praxis based on the assumptions of the theologian about embodiment. So the challenge is to find out the theologian's (half) conscious suppositions about the gendered body and its possibilities while doing and practicing practical theology. (2013, p. 66)

Althaus-Reid's 'per/versions' allow us to see 'a different version or understanding' (2004b, p. 107). When considering a queer understanding of practical theology, it becomes apparent there is a dearth of contributors, yet my journey through practical theology exposes the potentiality of sexuality to be part of the purpose and praxis of practical theology.

Therefore, critical engagement with sexual stories from non-normative lives is an act of practical theology. With the aim of que(e)rying the relationship of practical theology with sexual theology, I argue that a critical examination of the work of theologian Ruard Ganzevoort allows a more fruitful interpretation of practical theology for the purposes of exploring biographies and beliefs from sexual perverts, using the term in the same sense as Rubin, above.

Undoing Theology with Perverts

Viviane Namaste queries the validity of discussions about the complex nature of gender while the researcher occupies a safe place within academic ivory towers. She advocates a grounded research methodology in which the participants set the agenda for research production and knowledge transfer. Her title is a deliberate play on Butler's book *Undoing Gender* (2004) and criticizes academics who write about 'the Transgender Question' from a theoretical position without 'a detailed contextual analysis of the different ways social relations of race, labor, and gender intersect' (2009, p. 2). She argues that 'the theoretical and political task at hand, then, is not one of undoing gender. What is required is nothing short of undoing theory' (2009, p. 28).

Within her article, Namaste makes explicit references to previous research conducted with indigenous communities, thus providing a framework for knowledge-production through effective collaborative research which benefits the individuals or communities who participate in the research (rather than being researched). Her three key principles of relevance, equity in partnership and ownership which should be considered in the production of practical theology when engaging with individual life stories.

The life stories of the protagonists document the undoing of theology for the individuals who offer their narratives. Yet, unlike previous life-story research, it is necessary to move beyond idealized notions that this task will 'provide a voice' for stories to be heard, as this can be misleading and raises questions to whose voice is being heard. Indeed, 'claims to voice are inadequate, perhaps even misleading' (Bullough and Pinnegar, 2001, p. 17).

Althaus-Reid expresses a similar concern to Namaste but in relation to queer theologies as they 'are sometimes accused of being ungrounded, or not from the people' (2001a, p. 60). In addition to responding to Althaus-Reid's injunction to uncover sexual stories, it is important to follow Namaste's principle that 'feminist theory would be well served by actually speaking with everyday women about their lives' (2009, p. 27), as attending attentively to the stories of non-normative people is a practical theological task. A perversion of practical theology thus attends to the distinctive stories of those who have experienced the cumulative impact of heteronormative religious practice.

Althaus-Reid's 'perv's theology of ethics' (2004b, p. 106) invites us to imagine alternative sexual options on which we can base our theologies. Althaus-Reid, like Namaste, reminds us of the importance of partnership which is applicable to practical theological enquiry. She adopts the terminology of 'consensuality' as her first per/version and reminds us that 'queer theology is a theology of alliances in agreement with their own diversity' (2004b, p. 107). In her second per/version, Althaus-Reid reiterates her call for theologians to find the alternative sexual stories as a basis for forming theology:

> We start our reflections from our own sexual stories. We lift God's skirts after having lifted our own first. In lifting our skirts we remind ourselves of our own identity at the moment of doing theology while we remain committed to theological honesty. It is from an alliance of sexual epistemologies in disagreement with heterosexual ideology and not vice versa that we reflect on grace, redemption and salvation. (2004b, p. 107)

Part One: Queering Practical Theology

> Practical theology is especially suited to make contributions to church thought and practice by engaging in debates about sexuality and gender arising out of queer theory and practice. (Hoeft, 2012, p. 412)

Jeanne Hoeft's citation above is a rare example of how practical theology has engaged with sexuality. By rare, I am pointing to the dearth of discussions of sex and/or queer studies within practical theological literature. Hoeft's chapter entitled 'Gender, Sexism and Heterosexism' (2012) is a unique contribution to the field of pastoral theology, as she traces the theological lineage of (mostly) gender and (briefly) sexuality from feminist roots. Concerning herself with gender and sexual difference, she posits ways of '*doing gender*' [her emphasis] which are in keeping with Christian values (2012, p. 416). She notes how intersex-identifying individuals problematize simplistic categories of gender, and she observes how practical theology has shied away from a discussion of LGBT sexualities. Hoeft observes that 'there have been almost no queer identified texts from a practical or contextual perspective besides Althaus-Reid's' (2012, p. 419) as she encourages practical theologians to engage in discussions of sexuality and gender. Yet, her chapter raises an awareness of the issues of gender and sexuality, but she offers neither a methodology nor a response to how practical theology can serve to address such issues. Her conclusion serves solely to set out a gauntlet for others:

> Practical theologians must take up these questions and seek answers that account for the real people who struggle to find an authentic and meaningful life on the boundaries of church and society. (2012, p. 419)

Hoeft theorizes practical theology, but leaves it to others to deal with the messy task of investigating life stories. In this context, the praxis and methods of sexual storytelling is part of practical theology. Moreover, I claim that the objective and purpose of all theology is to make a difference; therefore, all theology should be based on *praxis*.

One further isolated example which documents the potentiality of practical theology to explore sexualized lives emerges in an essay from Kathleen Talvacchia (2015). Talvacchia questions the theory–practice divide for those who seek to gain an understanding of the theological and religious lived experiences of queer lives. Her essay explores an approach where theology is not a theoretical task, but one which also engages in a practical discovery of living religious experience. She notes:

> Practical theology done from a queer perspective ... has the potential to intentionally disrupt the binary of theory and practice in order to create an integrated approach in which the practices of queer religious communities and the theorizing about those practices can be more deeply in conversation with each other. (2015, p. 186)

Although critically congruent with the task of exploring non-normative lives in such terms, Talvacchia's approach is similar to Hoeft's. Within both essays the recognition of the potency of exploring non-normative experience as an act of practical theology is signposted. Nevertheless, both Talvacchia and Hoeft's positions are uncritically informed and neither provide concrete examples of how theological reflection on the lives of others could occur. Indeed, Talvacchia's own grounding of her practical theological approach is autobiographical, as she explores her own spiritual and sexual lives from a reflective theological lens. Thus, her method of theological reflection becomes an act of auto-theology, and arguably self-serving. Her theory–practical binary is only disruptive/disrupted in terms of making her own private self-reflections theologically public. Furthermore, as a trained academic theologian, her inclusion of autobiographical practical theology does not engage with the lives at the margins on a grassroots level, which is a necessary injunction for practical theology.

Therefore, a critical reading of practical theology serves to argue its potentiality for an exploration of sexual and theological praxis. To date, work on gender (almost exclusively from a feminist perspective[2]) can be found in practical theological literature, but practical theology has largely shied away from discussions of desire and intimacy, even within normative and heterosexual contexts. A paradigm shift within practical theology would enable it to realign itself with other important theoretical developments elsewhere in academic discourse.

Practical theologian Ruard Ganzevoort acknowledges and appreciates the large contribution feminist and pro-feminist theologians have made to gender studies within practical theology, yet he asks 'Adam, where are you?' (2011a, p. 1), puzzling as to where are the men contributing to gender studies in practical theology. Ganzevoort notes how Adam is absent, or mute, due to the fact that Adam is patriarchal and hegemonic. Outing Adam as a marked category of gender is just as important in challenging the dominant ideology and the sexual binary. Ganzevoort asks:

> Does [practical theology] still reflect the old structure of patriarchy in which only women (and maybe gay men) were supposed to have a gender, because men were the hegemonic and thus standard group who didn't have to reflect on their gender status? And where transgenders are invisible because they don't fit the binary? Just like 'people of color' includes people of all colors except the hegemonic white. Or like 'sexual diversity' seems to apply to all sexual varieties except heterosexuality. (2011a, p. 1)

Ganzevoort does not wish to dilute the work of feminist theology; rather he would like the spotlight to shine equally on other players including men, heterosexuals, transgender and the sexually adventurous of all orientations and inclinations. In his one brief mention of queer theology, Ganzevoort states that this endeavour must seek to explore 'underprivileged or subjugated groups and aim at their emancipation' (2011a, p. 3). Interestingly, Ganzevoort extends this by pointing to an exploration of the biographies of such individuals as a 'starting point in the acknowledgment of subjectivity' (2011a, p. 3).

Theology is done by embodied human beings, and embodiment is gendered and sexual. A sexual practical theology will use these gendered and sexual subjectivities as a starting point for Christians who have experienced shame and fear because of their sexual desires and practices. Embedded Christian imaginings of God are thus problematized as we examine our own bodies and experiences as a starting point to be suspicious of the dominant Christian tradition.

So, what would this perverted practical theology look like? Fulkerson, citing Charles Winquist, speaks of practical theology as 'a response to a wound' (2007, p. 2). Non-normative sexualities are scarred with the fallout from hegemonic understandings of compulsory heterosexuality. Leanne Tigert (1999) discusses how non-normative sexualities are often perceived as a scar, and that there is a trauma of homophobia in the lives of those who identify as non-heterosexual. This notion of trauma should also be extended to all non-normative lives, not just non-heterosexuals: identifying and staying in or coming out as non-normative can be a traumatic experience, one which can be painful. A perversion of practical theology would be to discuss openly sexual experiences in relation to one's self and faith understanding. It serves as a response to dominant ideologies from powerful Christian groups, such as churches. It is unlikely that sex is what Elaine Graham has in mind as she states, 'the task of practical theology itself is facilitating a creative dialogue between tradition and experience, theology and practice' (2013, p. 163), yet the tenets of practical theology do allow for the inclusion of all sexualities. Graham credits practical theologians as 'bearers of "living Christian tradition" which evolves in dialogue with contemporary experience' (2013, p. 163). As such, non-normative theologians form a discipleship:

> Practical theologians working within an action research paradigm commit themselves to nurturing ordinary people's autonomous and lived apprehensions of God as the well-spring of practical discipleship. (Graham, 2013, p. 177)

Sadly, Graham does not qualify what she means by 'ordinary' here. Yet, practical theology would not demand a significant shift in its praxis to widen its parameters to include non-*ordinary* people. Its praxis remains the same, yet its principles are extended to those on the margins. Attending to those on the margins of a traditional Christian understanding of sexuality is an entirely appropriate task for theology. What such a move will mean in practice can be seen in the contribution Ruard Ganzevoort has made to practical theology, as he advocates life stories as part of its praxis.

Ruard Ganzevoort: Life Stories as Practical Theology

The work of Ruard Ganzevoort has been instrumental in the development of a narrative approach to practical theology. Having published widely on life stories as a foundational starting point to theological discussions, he locates life stories within practical theology and acknowledges religion as part of lived experience. It is significant to note that his earlier work originates at the same time queer theory was emerging from academic closets, although he makes no reference to this in his work.

Ganzevoort's work on life stories is largely influenced by Anton Boisen's notion of the 'living human document'. Boisen said, 'we need to learn to read human documents as well as books' (1936, p. 10), which according to Ganzevoort signifies that the written narrative of a person's life can be 'studied in similar ways to the written documents of the Bible and ancient texts' (Ganzevoort, 1993, p. 285). This hermeneutical approach can be readily adopted by theologians and biblical scholars, who are already trained in literary and structural exegesis, according to Ganzevoort. He states that it is the 'expertise of theologians as interpreters of the stories in which the most fundamental questions of faith and meaning may come to the fore' (1993, p. 286).

Ganzevoort articulates the notion of storytelling as hermeneutics of self: 'a story is not just a way of conveying information, it is a way of interpreting facts' (1993, p. 277). He rightly defines life stories as 'narrative patterns of interpretation whereby we seek to discover the sense, meaning and value of life and of the events occurring in it' (1993, p. 278). Ganzevoort sees identity as a product of our own self-interpretation. He states, 'we do not just have a personal narrative, we are a narrative identity' (1993, p. 281).

How life stories can connect to practical theology relies on hermeneutics. For Ganzevoort, praxis and interpretation are intertwined. Simply, hermeneuts do not engage with biblical texts solely from the perspective of a believer. Theologians without any commitment or allegiance to Christianity are still investigating God and experiences of God, as 'whatever practical theologians may investigate, it is always connected in some way to human discourse in relation to God' (2002, p. 39). Theological thought thus emerges out of reflections and interpretations of human actions and interactions.

We have always interpreted our world through the stories we tell. In the production of a life story, Ganzevoort notes, 'certain events are experienced at an unconscious level, and afterwards are being interpreted and given a place in a narrative system' (1993, pp. 277–8). Therefore, life stories also contain one's self-understanding, one's sense of self and meaning of the events narrated. He makes an important observation in the production of 'living human texts', that once a story is told 'the narrative becomes text, in a certain sense detached from a person' (1993, p. 279). That is to say that in telling a story, there is a self-editing process in which an individual decides what to share and what to keep hidden. He observes that a 'shared story is not the same as the inner story. In telling the personal narrative, the narrator modifies the story' (1993, p. 278).

Elizabeth Spelman (1988) has famously argued that (women's) identities are not like 'pop-beads' with variables such as class, sexuality, race, dis/ability and gender strung together, where each bead can be 'popped off' for an analysis that suits the hypothesis of the researcher. Equally, narratives cannot be seen as separate items, similar to Spelman's 'pop-beads'. Stories can be told and heard in isolation, but it must be remembered that they always intertwine with other narratives. Narratives relate to one another because both the events they recall and the actors within the plot are shared across the production of other narratives:

> We do not write the personal narrative in a relational vacuum. For every individual there is a range of relationships within the social context. The personal narrative touches the narratives of others. We play a role in each other's story, and we contribute to a 'shared story' (especially in a community of faith). (Ganzevoort, 1993, p. 278)

This connects Ganzevoort's work on narrative with Judith Butler's perspective: that narratives are not just self-created or self-fashioned, but identity is also placed upon us. The dichotomy of internal narrative and external narrative (that is narrative identities we are called to create and produce) are not easily extrapolated.

Bonnie Miller-McLemore follows this basic principle of reading 'living human documents' but offers an additional point for consideration. Writing from a space which does not engage critically with Ganzevoort, she suggests a move away from studying individuals as living human documents and offers a significant new paradigm shift in which individuals are no longer read, but listened to, as part of a 'living human web' (1996). This, according to Miller-McLemore, stresses the 'interconnectivity of selfhood' (1996, p. 7). The matrix for human stories is relational and contextual. No one tells a story of their life with themselves as the only character. The interpretation of one's location within the 'living human web' is central to one's positionality and emerging identity. Accordingly, Ganzevoort states that life stories are both 'polyphonic' (2001, p. 46) and 'a multi-conversational discipline' (2002, p. 34).

I follow Ganzevoort who asserts that 'practical theology's possibilities and challenges lie in the specific conversations it engages in' (2002, p. 35). Stephen Pattison goes further than this, stating that critical conversations are a form of practical theology. In establishing a concrete model for such critical conversations to take place, he states:

> Practical theology can then be thought of as a critical conversation between aspects and interpretations of (a) one's own ideas, beliefs, experiences, feelings, perceptions and assumptions; (b) the beliefs, perceptions and assumptions arising from the Christian community and tradition (c) the contemporary situation, practice or event which is under consideration; and (d) relative insights, methods and findings that emerge from non-theological disciplines. (2000, pp. 9–10)

Pattison's model is a useful theoretical starting point to describe the critical conversations that emerge from sexual stories as an act of practical theology. To subject sexual experiences to a practical theological enquiry is to engage in a critical conversation between what is known and understood as contemporary sexual practices and experiences, alongside relevant aspects of Christian theology and tradition. Practical theology is therefore interdisciplinary. If practical theology has been blind to sexual stories and especially those from sexual migrants, then its possibilities have been severely constrained by its failure to engage in critical conversations. It is time for practical theology to stop shying away from talking about sex.

Narrative approaches, according to Ganzevoort, are thus performative rather than representative. Echoing Judith Butler's famous assertion that gender is performative, Ganzevoort highlights the inner-construction of identity which is performed once we engage in the production of life storytelling. Butler's position helps to highlight the complexities of life-story research, as she is 'permanently troubled by identity categories, consider[ing] them to be invariable stumbling blocks, [she] understand[s] them, even promote[s] them, as sites of necessary trouble' (Butler, 1991, p. 14). As gender is interwoven with narrative, Butler is not quite right to separate the pop-bead identity category of gender as performative. There are various other markers of identity that are performative when exposed through self-narration, just as religious identity can be equally performative.

Trauma and Theology

A further discussion of the nature of practical theology, informed by Ganzevoort, is based around his work on religious coping and trauma (1998a; 1998b; 2008), particularly in his earlier studies on sexually abused men. As noted earlier, non-normative 'outing' or even the internalization of non-normative sexual practice can be traumatic to the individual. This follows Tigert's notion of homophobia as traumatic and builds on the idea that practical theology is the response to a wound, or scar. Ganzevoort articulates a 'theology of trauma' (2008, p. 19). He reminds us that it is not a significant event in our lives which is traumatic, but the impact this event has on the individual: 'trauma [is] essentially a threat to identity. The central issue here is that traumatization interrupts the person's life course' (2008, p. 21).

In her publication of *Undoing Gender*, Butler links loss, and trauma and the effect this has on one's self-narrative. She states, 'trauma takes its toll on narrativity' (2004, p. 138). But, despite this interruption and toll, Ganzevoort notes how traumatic events 'define our identity' (2008, p. 24).

For non-normative sexual migrants, the scar of the alien landscape of vanilla heteronormativity is worn as a symbol of resistance. Resistance to heteronormative discourse has always been a feature of queer theory, with its intent to challenge assimilation politics in terms of sexuality. In such terms, Goss observes 'a gay/lesbian liberation theology begins with resistance and moves to political insurrection' (1993, p. xvii). It is therefore the work of practical theology to attend to the wounds of individuals who are marginalized because of whom they choose to love and how they choose to express their love. These marginalized voices are, in turn, empowered because a purpose is given to tell their stories to readers. These 'local stories … challenge the dominant logic of an oppressive society' (Ganzevoort, 2011b, p. 218) and the hegemonic, heteronormative interpretation of religion held by traditional theology.

Attending to One Another

> For every theology is always a sexual theology and it is necessary to uncover not just the gender codes but the sexual (ideological) assumptions of Christian theology, ecclesiology and the methods of theological inquiry which have pervaded our understanding of Christianity. (Althaus-Reid, 2004a, p. 4)

Although described as 'a practical theologian' by Bons-Storm (2013, p. 66), Althaus-Reid's contribution to theology based on sexuality, poverty and exclusion can be deduced from her notion of theology as a 'walk', or 'caminata'. This caminata involves the community and the locality. It is not a walk in isolation, but a walk in dialogue, which 'comes from the desire to have a coherent, liberative praxis in our thinking/doing of theology' (Althaus-Reid, 2004a, p. 14). For Althaus-Reid, this praxis of theology does not promote 'a hierarchy of knowledge' (2004a, p. 14) and does not bear witness to "'professional theologians" versus "people's theology"' (2004a, p. 14). There is no existent hierarchy between grassroots theology and academic theology, both are mutually complementary.

John Rowan's chapter 'The Humanistic Approach to Action Research' (2005) explores the spiritual undertaking of exploring one's own experience. He states, 'this is the basic attitude of the mystic in all religious traditions – to get inside one's own experience, to commit oneself to one's own experience, to trust one's own experience' (2005, p. 108). In the context of theology, rather than the social sciences, the sharing of experience can be essentially a spiritual undertaking. This is, however, nothing new. Previously, Pierre Bourdieu had described the ethics of listening as 'intellectual love' (1999, p. 614). Barbara McClure (2008) developed the motif of 'attending to one another' as a basis for pastoral theology. This attention relies on a committed vocation of listening and waiting in order to hear fully another's story. McClure describes 'attending' as creating 'temporal space for God, truth, mystery, the sacred, to present itself. It presupposes the possibilities of new realities breaking forth' (2008, p. 191). Elaine Graham, extending McClure's approach, states:

> 'attending' is a matter of both action *and* reflection. It synthesizes a pastoral role of being present and mindful of the needs and well-being of the other, with an openness to new insights that transcend functional consideration. (2013, p. 176)

In the matter of attending to one another, Eileen Campbell-Reid and Christian Scharen offer a rationale 'for making use of silence as a key aspect of theological ethnography' (2013, p. 232). Their article, 'Ethnography on Holy Ground: How Qualitative Interviewing is Practical Theological Work', describes the interview space in theological action research as a 'safe and holy space' (2013, p. 243). Telling their own stories in the space allowed 'God's creative and graceful presence to be discovered' (2013, p. 254). So, for the Christian narrators who share them, God is creatively revealed in the process of telling them.

Campbell-Reid and Scharen adopt the metaphor of the graceful conduct of exchanging life stories as 'holding a small bird' (2013, p. 245), describing a potential space in which participants mutually hold one another, thus participating in 'the sacred character of making space for being seen, heard and recognized' (2013, p. 247). This space seeks to engender trust while acknowledging the fragility of human relationships. It prioritizes 'the intimacy and empathy of genuinely attending to one another' (2013, p. 245). Attending to one another represents the respect and honour one gives to others: their stories, their time and their beliefs.

From a counselling perspective, to adopt the principle of 'attending to one another' without undercurrents of power differentials, the idea of 'being with' is an important model within a person-centred approach to therapy. Therefore, the analogy of holding a small bird could seem patronizing to the narrator and this also raises the questions of relationship dynamics between storyteller and listener. Therefore, moving away from this ornithological analogy, it is more helpful to consider an attitude of unconditional positive regard towards the narrator. Mark Harrison reflects on the concept of 'being with' and a non-directive approach to attending to others, and he relates this directly to the passion of Christ. He asks, 'in his "being-with" those who crucified him, did Jesus show the greatest acceptance of the "serious harm" that would then occur?' (2012, p. 23). This unconditional positive regard for one another is exemplified by Harrison within Jesus's own actions in 'being with' those around him, attending to them and preparing them for what was to come after Jesus's final hours.

On Giving and Receiving

The metaphor of giving and receiving can be a sexual one, largely based on sanctioned and sanctified heterosexual practices where the male gives and the female receives. Binaries of activism/passivism, top/bottom and giver/receiver are pairings that sterilize the notion of sex as mutually fulfilling, irrespective of the assigned roles of either participant. I mentioned previously that it is important to avoid categorizations, and this too applies to a consideration of the role of storyteller as 'giver' or listener as 'receiver'. I appreciate Clifford Geertz's adoption of a sexual metaphor in relation to the sharing of oneself, 'you don't exactly penetrate another culture, as the masculinist image would have it. You put yourself in its way and it bodies forth and enmeshes you' (1995, p. 44). The researcher here is more open and reflexive than one who seeks to adopt a position which is ontologically stable and objective.

It is vital to remember that the production of sexual stories as a form of theology is dependent on the help of others. There must be a strong sense of trust to be able to share and explore the intricacies of a person's life. Jamie Heckert narrates his own feelings of exploitation when conducting what he terms 'queer research' with others:

> I was often more concerned with giving than receiving. I have a memory of expressing concern to one of my research partners that I might be exploiting them by taking their stories. She reminded me that by listening, I was giving something as well. Giving and receiving, receiving and giving: an anarchist economics of research and a compassionate queering of borders between self and other. (2010, p. 51)

Perverting practical theology adopts the method of '*caminata*', of 'being with' or 'going with' participants as they share their experiences. It is a relationship process which can be described as similar to sexual practices with another individual. It involves attending to one another with sensitivity and intuition. It embraces intimacy, creating a relationship based on mutual respect and a sacred reverence of one another. It is consensual, in which boundaries are negotiated and roles are mutually fulfilling. Can such a perverted practical theology be considered a sexual encounter? It is an encounter between minds channelled through the sharing of stories and experiences which is certainly based on the relationality of sex.

Part Two: 'Undoing' Queer Theory

The Queer I/Eye

Martin Stringer states 'all writers on sexual matters have to contextualize themselves and their writing' (1997, p. 27). The need to provide personal demographic information emerges from feminist scholarship, in what Nancy Miller terms as 'the obligatory dance cards of representivity' (1991, p. 121). Miller notes the introduction to such contextualization often begins with 'the waltz of the *as a*' (1991, p. 121), as scholars prefix their self-representation with 'as a ...' Accordingly, here I consider my personal stake in this work, including my own questioning of the validity of queer research.

My first concern relates to the task of utilizing sexual storytelling as a theological framework. Deryn Guest observes how an exploration of personal testimonies 'can be dismissed as "labours of love" or an unnecessary "baring of the soul" that is slightly embarrassing and best left to the private sphere' (2005, pp. 235–6). Similarly, Robert Goss additionally observes the threat of such work being sidelined:

> Queer postmodern theologians are marginalized because they threaten the very gender and sexual codes upon which those master religious narratives have been constructed. (1999, p. 48)

Guest revisits this idea of queer as academically marginalized and an indulgence in her later work (2012). She reassures queerists that it 'is not about adopting a cool, hip, academic identity; it is about embarking upon serious, detailed work on heteronormativity and the heterosexual imaginary' (2012, p. 161).

My second concern is that, although queer is marginalized, as noted by Guest, its impact as a theory must be mobilized in order for it to have import beyond the academy. This is also taken up by Guest who notes how queer theory 'will prove to be an elitist discourse, hardly accessible to the lay person or in touch with the lived realities of the grassroots communities' (2005, p. 51). Guest's concern is that queer theory may not engage with the realities of lives and experiences of those who identify as non-normative. She notes how 'the level of political engagement here is worryingly low' (2005, p. 48), and she is not alone in sharing such unease around the use of *queer*. Indeed, Guest's references to Rich (1980), Escoffier (1990) and Malinowitz (1993) exemplify further examples of discomfort. Five years later, Sally Munt holds on to the same concern:

So, the extraordinary and creative queer theory of universities, which values discomfort and disruption, and that valenced term 'unhinged', often has limited applicability when perceived by non-academic LGBTQI people. (2010, p. 23)

What these concerned scholars rightly identify as disquiet around the term *queer* actually highlights the importance of conducting queer research on the ground. Encouraging people to share their stories enables us to uncover and examine the religious, social and political oppression faced by individuals and groups that have historically been marginalized. This, in turn, serves to challenge Christian theological traditions and to counter the discriminatory doctrines, dogmas and theologians that produced them.

That said, academic theorizing remains an important component to the project, not only as its starting point, but to ensure the required intellectual rigour and credibility. Queer theology has not always successfully engaged with critical queer theory, as observed by Susannah Cornwall, which has resulted in its less credible status as an academic discipline:

Interestingly queer theologians have often not engaged explicitly in their writing with Butler, Foucault and the other theorists whose work underlines queer theory ... if queer theologians do not use the term in the same way that queer critical theorists do, this may make queer theology less credible as an intellectual discourse. (2011, p. 24)

So, there needs to be balance between using the academic tools of queer theory, while remaining accountable to the primary constituents it originally served, especially those who identify as non-normative. This project explores how non-normative sexualities can serve as a basis to theologize from an experiential perspective. Moreover, I move beyond minoritized sexualities and genders to encompass straight-identified individuals who engage in 'queer' sexual practices. In order to achieve this, I focus attention on how queer is a transformational force.

The queer 'I' is a prominent feature of my understanding of self-as-researcher. Althaus-Reid and Isherwood encourage first person discourse: 'as a genre, queer theology partakes of the irony, humour and self-disclosure type of discourse … Queer theology is an "I" theology' (2004, p. 6). Koosed agrees, 'by using autobiographical language ("I"), the text poses as an interface between the author and the reader' (2006, p. 342). This queer 'I' therefore embraces and advocates the use of personal testimonies as a significant part of queer theological discourse.

Positioning of Self

It is therefore appropriate now for me to disclose my location and self-understanding. In addition to the opening tale of my childhood which introduced this book, I offer the following self-description. I am a cis-gendered male, who was assigned male at birth, and I am in a monogamous civil partnership with another male. Although my work seeks to evade categories of identity, I do self-identify as a gay man. Indeed, in seeking to avoid binary categorizations of identity, there may seem an inherent contraction in stating I am a gay male. This contradiction is not unique to me. Koosed notes the complexities and inconsistencies of locating oneself: 'I see the inconsistencies of my own identity; the contradictions of my own sexed and gendered self' (2006, p. 342). Notwithstanding, my work welcomes those who prefer not to be limited by binary gender categorizations. To some extent, the self-disclosure of my sexuality influences, informs and arguably provides a catalyst for my identity as a queer sexual theologian.

However, the queer 'I' and the queer 'eye' recognize different locations and positions: the sharing of sexual stories is a personal undertaking, and attending to those stories can be equally personal. I acknowledge that I can never fully adopt the position of 'insider' to others' stories (Merton, 1972). On the one hand, I could be treated as an insider, my sexuality is non-normative and therefore I am somewhat of an ally to others' stories of deviance. However, on the other hand, I am also an outsider, as others' experiences are unique to them. Throughout my research, I am both observer (eye) and personally intertwined (I).

Concerning my religious identity, this is more a fluid and hybrid status which is a challenge to define. Happy is the religious mongrel who needs not select a category of identification! Biographically, I grew up in a large Roman Catholic family in the north of England and was educated within comprehensive Catholic schooling until the age of 18. In addition to a long, passionate yet broken relationship with Catholicism, I have flirted with atheism, Methodism and Pentecostalism, and I have been known to frequent Church of England services too. I do not practise any religion formally, though I do pray occasionally. I adore my numerous Buddha statues at home and appreciate my partner's creative 'dragging' up of Catholic iconic statues that adorn our home.

Jennie Barnsley advocates the use of gender-neutral pronouns, using 'per' to replace what in binary terms has served as the third person possessive pronouns 'his/her'. In per unpublished PhD thesis, Jennie Barnsley describes perself as 'non-Christian' as 'the description non-Christian does not situate [per] outside of Christian theology, since Christianity is at the very heart of [per] non-Christian theologising' (2013, p. 87). My own personal heritage is Christian, and my experiences are situated within Christian beliefs, doctrines and practices, yet my theologies are not traditional Christian teachings, therefore I could situate myself along the spectrum between identifying as non-Christian and post-Christian. Sally Munt describes post-Christian discourse and rhetoric as 'no longer rooted in the languages and assumptions of Christianity' (2010, p. 9). It is arguably the constraints of heteronormativity within my Christian experiences which empower me to theologize queerly and to go in search of non-normative life stories to enable others to do the same. Such constraints provide a catalyst for theological activism.

This subjective autobiographical account of my position as researcher is not an indulgent self-promoting narrative. Ross Mooney's pioneering text about the importance of the researcher's viewpoint reminds us that research is hardly ever a neutral process: 'research is a personal venture which, quite aside from its social benefits, is worth doing for its direct contribution to one's own self-realization' (1957, p. 155). More recently, Bullough and Pinnegar summarize this idea judiciously: 'who a researcher is, is central to what a researcher does' (2001, p. 13).

Queer Theory and Theology

In his chapter, 'Queer Theory, Hermeneutics and the Limits of Libertinism' (2010) Graham Ward's commendation of Althaus-Reid's impact on theology leaves an unexpected twist. Ward leaves queerists aghast with his assertion 'we still await a queer theory' (2010, p. 168). His reasoning for such a statement is that 'queering does not allow for the theoretical standpoint; it does not permit a methodology' (2010, p. 168). He is among thinkers who argue it cannot be permitted to have a methodology or standpoint precisely because it would then no longer be 'queer' – it has to be nomadic, fluid, unclassifiable, or it is assimilated and de-clawed. It is interesting Ward makes this comment in the same year as Browne and Nash publish their volume entitled *Queer Methods and Methodologies* (2010). Browne and Nash state:

> Many scholars who use queer theorisations can use undefined notions of what they mean by 'queer research' and rarely undertake a sustained consideration of how queer approaches might sit with (particularly social scientific) methodological choices. In research deemed 'queer', the methods we use often let us speak to or interact with people, usually on the basis of sexual/gender identities and within anti-normative frameworks. (2010, p. 1)

In seeking to uncover the kinship of quasi-queer methodologies, I first look at two examples based on the work of Althaus-Reid and Karen E. Macke.

First, Althaus-Reid would see *outing theology* as a methodology that produces queer theology: 'queer theology is a process of Outing Theology as a method for action and reflection' (2001a, p. 60). 'Outing' functions as a verb often associated with making hypocrites visible, with its roots in homophobic pronouncements from people who have engaged in same-sex activities. Here, however, Althaus-Reid is referring to voluntary outing. Such *outing*, she argues, depends upon the sharing of sexual narratives: 'in Queer Theology, coming out as a hermeneutical circle works well by telling sexual stories as a base of doing a popular Queer theology' (2001a, pp. 64–5).

Second, Karen E. Macke distinguishes between 'queering' and 'que(e)rying': 'where "queering" is more usefully seen as a goal of inquiry driven by queer theory, "que(e)rying" denotes a methodology, or a strategy driving qualitative research' (2014, p. 16). Within Macke's approach, queer research based on 'que(e) rying' will always be anchored in methodology, a methodology that requires us to define our research and erect boundaries, frameworks and other scientific tools to impose rigour. This is problematic for the queer researcher. Thankfully, Jamie Heckert's more fluid approach of 'becoming-queer' permits the researcher to work with what emerges organically.

On 'Becoming-Queer'

How honest, how daring, could I be . . .? How queer can one be in a university? (Heckert, 2010, p. 42)

Heckert's own research paradigm signposts an unorthodox methodology in qualitative research, which he describes as 'becoming-queer' (2010, p. 43). Much ink has been spilt in discussing the term 'queer', yet Heckert's term 'becoming-queer'

sidesteps any efforts to make queer into a new disciplinary category. It takes the power out of the voices asking 'am I queer enough? Is she really queer?' No one IS queer. Anyone might be becoming-queer. (2010, p. 43)

Heckert details how a 'becoming-queer' methodology relinquishes control of hypotheses, or rigid methodological plans. This follows the path paved by postmodernist theory in antagonizing academic norms. With reference to postmodernist scholarship, Heckert draws on the work of Giles Deleuze and Felix Guattari (1994; 1999; 2000). Heckert narrates his own research journey, where he investigated sexual orientation and the erosion of identity labels, and he describes the issues and emotions he experienced when conducting qualitative research for his doctoral studies. In one example, he writes:

> I have a memory of my supervisor asking me why I was so sure these stories would be suitable for my research. I wasn't sure and I couldn't explain to him why I wanted to do this. Listening to my own intuition, I was making a queer methodological choice. (2010, p. 45)

He describes his approach as one where 'the theoretical development of the work, not simply as illustrations of high theory, but as theoretically sophisticated in themselves' (2010, p. 48). This is contrary to traditional theory-led investigations. Heckert's 'becoming-queer' methodology is one which – although aware of binary borders: theory/data; researcher/researched; hetero/homo; right/wrong (2010, p. 43) – the lines are blurred. This 'becoming-queer' methodology has principles I embrace, yet I suggest a shift in nomenclature based on the work of Judith Butler.

Judith Butler: Doing and Undoing

During the 1990s, Butler pioneered a critical shift within the domain of gender and sexual theory, with the publication of *Gender Trouble* (1990) and *Bodies That Matter* (1993). Her significant contribution to queer theory enabled an understanding of gender as a performative identity. She sees the norms which govern gendered identity as a social construct:

> Gender ought not to be construed as a stable identity of locus of agency from which various acts follow; rather gender is an identity tenuously constituted in time, instituted in an exterior space through a *stylized repetition of acts [sic]*. (Butler, 1990, p. 191)

> Gender is the repeated stylization of the body, a set of repeated acts within a highly rigid regulatory frame that congeal over time to produce the appearance of substance, of a natural sort of being.

A political genealogy of gender ontologies, if it is successful, will deconstruct the substantive appearance of gender into its constitutive acts and locate and account for those acts within the compulsory frames set by the various forces that police the social appearance of gender. (1990, p. 45)

Put in less opaque terms, gender can be viewed as culturally enforced and driven by compulsory heterosexuality. Such gender norms are powerful only because they have been established and are repeated. Thus, gendered identity is brought about and perpetuated through its own repetition. Gender performativity is not simply putting on a conscious identity on a day-to-day basis, but there is compunction about it, and the individual becomes gendered through this (un)conscious repetition of gendered accessories and behaviours. Butler labels this performativity as compulsive because individuals subconsciously seek to conform because it is practically impossible to break free entirely:

Performativity describes this relation of being implicated in that which one opposes, the turning of power against itself to produce alternative modalities of power. (1993, p. 241)

Butler warns that performativity should not be confused with performance. Whereas the latter is dramatic, light-hearted and entertaining, the former is compulsory and forced upon individuals through 'the forces of prohibition and taboo, with the threat of ostracism and even death' (1993, p. 95). She continues, noting how performative signifiers are not under individual control, rather they form part of a collective significance:

The reach of their signifiability cannot be controlled by the one who utters or writes, since such productions are not owned by the one who utters them. They continue to signify in spite of their authors, and sometimes against their authors' most precious intentions. (1993, p. 241)

To expose such signifiers as arbitrary constructs, Butler asserts that we must subvert such gendered norms in order to break the power of repetition. Thus, in suggesting that gender is an unstable concept, she observes that within the performativity there is also an inbuilt interval between the compulsory, repetitive re-enactments that create and maintain the illusions of identity, and this is the potential site of disruption. Ken Stone summarizes this neatly, noting how the repeated acts of gender are '(re)installed as norms; and they come to seem quite solid and substantial. Yet there are differences, gaps, moments of confusion, and multiple possibilities for meaning among these citations' (2007, p. 192).

To illustrate the act of subversion of gender norms, Butler uses the example of a drag queen to highlight the performative nature of gender. She argues how this exposes the instability of gender and the performative nature of identities which are interpreted in binary terms as masculine or feminine. Essentially, drag queens parody gender, mimicking normative assumptions about gender. Drag exposes and disrupts the arbitrary foundations on which social and cultural gender assumptions are made.

One of Butler's most significant claims was her argument about the arbitrary foundations on which heterosexuality is constructed, as gender and heterosexuality are arguably firmly grounded on a social level. Daniel Warner simplifies the notion of the performativity of gender:

> Consider this: of all the men you interact with on a daily basis, how many of their penises have you ever really inspected for biological authenticity? Do we not usually just presume their existence and move on from there? In practice, judgements of gender identity are based on public performances, not private parts. (2004, p. 324)

In *Undoing Gender* Butler describes the *doing* of gender, before calling for its *undoing:*

> If gender is a kind of a doing, an incessant activity performed, in part, without one's knowing and without one's willing, it is not for that reason automatic or mechanical. On the contrary, it is a practice of improvisation within a scene of constraint. Moreover, one does not 'do' one's gender alone. One is always 'doing' with

or for another, even if the other is only imaginary. (2004, p. 1)

To consider oneself as an individual agent is false, according to Butler. To be human is to be entwined in relations with others, as noted in my account of Miller-McLemore's 'living human web' in Part One of this chapter. Our connections with others are involuntary; we have no choice in our susceptibility to others: 'Let's face it, we're undone by each other. And if we are not, we're missing something' (Butler, 2004, p. 19).

Although put in rather negative terms, remaining within the complexity of Butler's understanding of human relations is significant in order to articulate a platform for 'undoing' theology. Butler substantiates the notion of 'undoing' in acknowledging the 'doing': 'we must be undone in order to do ourselves: we must be part of a larger social fabric of existence in order to create who we are' (2004, pp. 100–01). As we acknowledge that our identities and life stories are relationally produced, Butler wants us to consider in what ways we are 'undone'. To whom do we have attachments, responsibilities, connections?

Butler cites grief and desire as two of the factors by which we are connected and vulnerable towards others (2004, p. 19). Although Butler does not refer directly to any desire for connectivity with the divine, her notions of creation, existence and social relationality discussed above can be translated into theological terms. Desiring God and desire for engaging in non-normative sexual practices are processes by which my participants are 'undone'. Therefore, a Butlerian approach would require theology to be 'undone' too.

Breaking the Habits: Unbecoming and Undoing

E. L. McCallum and Mikka Tuhkanen substantiate Heckert's advocacy of a queer-becoming: 'if queer theorists have agreed on anything, it is that, for queer thought to have any specificity at all, it must be classified by becoming, the constant breaking of habits' (2011, p. 10). This idea of a 'constant breaking of habits' suggests an interruption to the repetition of acts. A theory of 'becoming-queer' attempts to subvert the repetition of acts: it breaks the cycle, the norms, and this rupture becomes uncategorizable. Yet, to cite 'becoming' as a queer process suggests an established model of queer, introducing its own cycle and norms. Once an attempt to reify how to 'do' queer has been explained, it actually no longer becomes queer. It no longer recognizes the need to break habits and repetition; dangerously, it attempts to categorize queer. McCallum and Tuhkanen point out that 'becoming becomes notably un-queer, describing an orthodox relation between subject and its context: queer is nothing if not improper, unfitting, unsuitable' (2011, p. 10).

Therefore, in building upon Heckert's 'becoming-queer' stance, I argue that we must equally balance this with a conscious 'unbecoming' too. McCallum and Tuhkanen acknowledge the real personal challenges queer work presents:

> Butler opens up the space to think queer becoming as unbecoming, as a question of the lack of fit, the difficulties of interpretation, the moments of textual resistance or of unintelligibility that scholars ... wrestle with in their work. (2011, p. 10)

This raises the argument that it is perhaps un-queer to classify Heckert's 'becoming-queer' approach as a methodology. Methodology, as a systematic description of academic undertaking, is a word that smacks of order, rigour and process. Butler herself states, 'passions for foundations and methods sometimes get in the way of an analysis of contemporary political culture' (2004, p. 181), and this is true for queer practical theology.

Acknowledging 'becoming-queer' as a process of unbecoming too is therefore not so much a method, but a tapestry, interwoven and yet unthreaded. 'Becoming-queer' is connoted by a process where subjects constantly or performatively rework and reinvent their lack of fit while remaining embedded and conscious of the hegemonic binary. Thus, there are potential pitfalls to both Butler and Heckert's theorizing, which employs vocabulary that can be challenged by their antonyms such as 'becoming/unbecoming' 'queer/un-queer'. Antonymic couplings always point to the existence of binary positions which queer has attempted to subvert.

Butler's pivotal theorizing on *undoing* has methodological

considerations for the sharing of sexual stories as a source for undoing theology. There cannot be claims to 'do' theology in this way, as it requires to be 'undone'.

Queer Failure: Concern About Not Being 'Serious' Enough

> The temporary totalization performed by identity categories is a necessary error. And if identity is a necessary error, then the assertion of 'queer' will be necessary as a term of affiliation, but it will not fully describe those it purports to represent. As a result, it will be necessary to affirm the contingency of the term: to let it be vanquished by those who are excluded by the term but who justifiably expect representation by it. (Butler, 1993, p. 230)

According to Butler, as soon as queer is claimed to be representative of one group with a shared or collective identity, it excludes others. Each time it is claimed as representative of that group, it fails to be able to resist normativity. She talks about 'necessary failures' (1990, p. 199) due to 'a variety of incoherent configurations that in their multiplicity exceed and defy the injunction by which they are generated' (1990, p. 199). Similarly, Cornwall notes how queer is aware of its own shortcomings; 'failure, inadequacy and obsolescence are built into queer from the start' (2011, p. 15).

Thus, the notion of failure when 'undoing theology' based on queer paradigms is one which needs to be addressed. In *The Queer Art of Failure* (2011), Judith Halberstam recognizes the failings of queer and goes in search of some alternatives. The premise of her text is put in simple terms:

> Under certain circumstances, failing, losing, forgetting, unmaking, undoing, unbecoming, not knowing may in fact offer more creative, more cooperative, more surprising ways of being in the world. (2011, pp. 2–3)

The notion of queerness could therefore be built on conscious failure: a failure to conform or to belong. Halberstam's position is that queer should not be remoulded in order for us to seek to adapt to the model which fits all but none at the same time, but rather that we should accept failure willingly and enthusiastically, as it offers elements of surprise. Halberstam therefore offers 'low theory' to 'explore alternatives and to look for a way out of the usual traps and impasses of binary formulations' (2011, p. 2). The use of low theory serves as a critique to queer formulations which have claimed to break new ground but held on tight to conventional methods. Halberstam continues, 'low theory tries to locate all the in-between spaces that save us from being snared by the hooks of hegemony and speared by the seductions of the gift shop' (2011, p. 2).

Mobilizing low theory exposes itself to the possibility of not being credible or serious enough. Yet this is Halberstam's intention:

> Being taken seriously means missing out on the chance to be frivolous, promiscuous, and irrelevant. The desire to be taken seriously is precisely what compels people to follow the tried and true paths of knowledge production around which I would like to map a few detours. Indeed terms like *serious* and *rigorous* tend to be code words, in academia as well as other contexts, for disciplinary correctness; they signal a form of training and learning that confirms what is already known according to approved methods of knowing, but they do not allow for visionary insights or flights of fancy. (2011, p. 6)

Halberstam continues, 'Training of any kind, in fact … is about staying in well-lit territories and about knowing exactly which way to go before you set out. Like many others before me, I propose that instead the goal is to lose one's way' (2011, p. 6).

Accordingly, I express my desire to subvert the *doing* of theology by describing the sharing of sexual stories as part of a queer paradigm: an undoing of traditional theology. Fully aware of the inescapable binary of 'doing' and 'undoing', this form of theology subverts traditional approaches by undoing them, thus remaining a queer enterprise. By not following rigid processes with distinctive lines of enquiry, an undoing of theology is unbound and creative. It does not create or follow rules, nor search for concrete models. Butler states that the theoretical and political task at hand is one of *undoing gender*, Viviane Namaste states that the theoretical and political task is one of *undoing theory*. In combining both views here, I state that the task is *undoing theology*. In the three narrative chapters which follow, this task is accomplished through the sharing of intimate stories.

3

Intersex Bodies and Christianity
Alyce's Story

I am both male and female, although there are times I feel neither. One story is that I'm a man with breasts. The other story is that I'm a woman with a small penis.

Catholic guilt really is at the core of my gender issues. The Catholic Church I knew as a boy was not so much about doing good, it was more of what you shouldn't do. Everything was a sin, and if you sinned you went to hell.

Alyce inhabits the body of a 62-year-old presenting male, Jerry, who is heterosexual, married and has two adult daughters. They live in the United States. Alyce, however, is not the same age as Jerry. She states, 'I've created my own history, and one of the major differences is that Alyce is 20 years younger than Jerry.'

Intersex Bodies and Christianity

Intersex bodies are not always identifiable at birth, and some only become apparent during puberty. Intersex relates to external genitalia along a continuum rather than a binary. As well as affecting external genitalia such as testes and ovaries, it can also affect reproduction. It is estimated that 1 in 2,500 people experience what is medically termed as DSD – Disorders of Sex Development (Cornwall, 2010a, p. 2). Indeed, to describe intersex as a 'disorder' or 'condition' is a medical expression; individuals usually describe themselves as 'with intersex bodies'. Although Cornwall uses a slash to refer to intersex/DSD, Alyce did not use the term DSD at all in her interview. She used the terms 'intersex' or 'possible XXY', which are therefore the terms I use in describing her. More importantly, gender should not be reduced to chromosomes: it is a spectrum, a personal identity, a form of self-expression.

Alyce introduced herself as *XXY Catholic*, stating, 'The traditional viewpoint is that I'm a male, an XY with an additional X chromosome. That's the public life I've led. Had I been diagnosed, I'm sure they would have treated me with male hormones.' Intersex bodies are those where genitals, gonads, hormones or chromosomes are various, and do not line up with the perceived male/female binary. Chromosomes can vary along the combinations of XX (males), XY (females). Alyce identifies as XXY, which relates to a diagnosis of a male, with an underdeveloped penis and large breast tissue.

Although identifying as an intersex individual, Alyce presents publicly as male: Jerry. Jerry did not share his story with me; only Alyce communicated with me. For this reason, I use female pronouns (she/her), which she used to refer to herself. Initially, Alyce said she identifies as both male and female, yet in subsequent emails she said she 'suspect[s] some form of XXY condition', and it is apparent that there has been no real diagnosis. This does not suggest that Alyce's self-description of gender should be unstable because of its lack of medical confirmation. Indeed, as a marker of identity, it is the self-designation of an individual that is important. Susannah Cornwall has been a pioneer in the field of intersex bodies and Christian theology (2010a; 2013b; 2014; 2015). She notes how 'transpeople are expected to "test" their new gender [which] highlights the oddness of the fact that non-transpeople are not expected similarly to "try out" their gender roles before they are "confirmed"' (2010a, p. 111). She refers to the work of Johnson (2007) and expands this point with regard to sexuality, 'an individual who identifies as lesbian, gay or bisexual has no need to engage with the psychiatric profession in order to be able to pursue his or her lifestyle'. Cornwall continues, 'this points to an instance of sexuality appearing to be read as more essential or irreducible than gender identity' (2010a, p. 111).

Cornwall's leading work, *Sex and Uncertainty in the Body of Christ* (2010a) provided a full-length examination of intersex bodies and the theological implications of such complex gender. Nonetheless, by her own admission, this first text (2010a), although a positive theological account of intersex, '[has] not, to date, engaged in depth with intersex Christians' experiences or accounts of interactions between their intersex and Christian identities' (2014, p. 221).

Conscious of this lack of engagement with experience, which Cornwall later cites as a 'missing source' for theology (2015, p. 17), her two journal articles (2013b; 2014) are based on empirical research with ten self-identifying intersex individuals. Later, one of her book chapters (2015) addresses the thorny issue of experience, which has too often been considered 'too subjective, idiosyncratic, and distortion prone to be a robust source for theology' (2015, p. 154). In countering such problematic concerns, she asserts that 'eliding the category of experience compromises the agency and full personhood of intersex people' (2015, p. 18). Therefore, the aim of her chapter is to explore the experience of six intersex individuals as a basis for theological reflection. My purpose in presenting Alyce's story here is not to reiterate the ground-breaking research Cornwall has conducted, but to present, in more detail than Cornwall has previously afforded, the story of one intersex-identifying individual, exploring Alyce and Jerry's biographies and theologies.

Alyce in Genderland

The complexity of intersex results in a polyphonic narrative in this story, in which Alyce and Jerry's stories are intertwined, yet separate. Alyce states, 'even though I differentiate between me and him, I don't think we're two different people. I used to think he was the real ME, not anymore. I think I invented him, not the other way around.'

The dual narrative of Jerry/Alyce within this section does demonstrate a lack of cohesion and consensus. Alyce clarifies this point:

One point I'd like to make clear is that I am Alyce. Technically, I'm the pseudonym. I don't want you to think that there's some kind of 'Three Faces of Eve' thing going on in my head. It's not like that. I just believe that I am female in temperament and have been repressed all these years. The male persona was just a creation to match the genitalia. So if I refer to HIM, it's just my way of differentiating between the male and female personalities.

To illustrate this point of duality a little more clearly, the following example of the seemingly contradictory nature of a dual narrative is expressed when Alyce talks about her diet choices compared to those of Jerry. She discusses a meal out for Jerry's birthday:

After dinner, the waiter brought him a piece of Tiramisu (with a birthday candle) and a scoop of Italian ice cream. Jerry would never ever eat that, but I started picking at it without even thinking about it. I actually started eating different foods about a month ago. Things Jerry would never touch. Like yogurt. I seem to be much more open to trying different foods than he is. My diet is completely different than his.

What is significant about Alyce's observation is that although sharing embodiment, Alyce and Jerry have different tastes, physical desires and modes of physical expression. This results in what I term a 'duel of duality', which is explored in more detail later on. The term 'duel' smacks of conflict, and the episodes of Alyce's experiences narrated demonstrate clear differences and disagreements between Alyce and Jerry.

To continue with Alyce and Jerry's biography, attention now turns to the story of their childhood experiences – a story charged with emotion as Alyce narrates shame and suffering she experienced because of her complex gender.

Sin, Shame and Suffering: Childhood and Adolescent Experiences

Alyce was born and raised as a Catholic in the USA in the 1950s. As early as four or five years old, she recalls trying on her older sister's clothes when she was out, as they shared a bedroom. Alyce notes how the few early childhood memories she has seem to be connected to gender issues. She comments, 'I don't think I was an effeminate boy, but I always felt like I wanted to be a girl.' Alyce offers one of her earliest memories relating to gender and shame:

I remember my mother visiting a friend of hers, and she put a little makeup on me and let me put on her high heels. I remember her saying that I was too pretty to be a boy. My mother politely went along with it at first, but after a very short time, my mother lifted me up by my armpits and said we had to go.

Here's the ironic part, when I got older, around the 7th or 8th grade, I would rush to put on my mother's lipstick whenever she went out and left me alone. In the 8th grade I was in a St. Patrick's Day play at school, and the teacher instructed us to put lipstick on so that our mouth would be visible under the strong lighting. But rather than enjoy the opportunity to wear makeup in public, I didn't want to do it. As soon as the play was over, I was rubbing my lips as hard as I could, trying to remove it so that no one would see me on the way home. And we lived directly across the street from the school so it wasn't like I'd be exposed to hundreds of people. In fact, I think the only person that saw us during our two minute walk home was the doorman of our apartment building. I remember blurting out something like 'I was in a play, that's why I'm wearing lipstick.' The minute I got in the apartment, I ran to the bathroom to wash it off. For the next few days, I was convinced there was still some remaining.

Behind all of this was the notion that boys acting like girls was a 'sin'. If I held my sister's pocketbook for her, my mom would make me hand it back to her because it was a sin. When we visited relatives on Christmas, I wasn't allowed to play with my cousin if she was playing with her Barbie. It was a sin. Not a mortal sin, but a sin nonetheless. To this day, it is difficult for me to say bra or panties. Boys didn't say those things. It was sinful even think about them.

From a childhood littered with the notion of 'sin' relating to a feminization of her presenting gender, Alyce moved into adolescence, which was tormented with episodes of shame. Significantly and largely, this sense of shame was related to her own awareness of her physical appearance:

> When puberty came, I didn't grow strong and muscular, I grew breasts. My genitalia was male, but very small.

Alyce's recounting of adolescent years are filled with memories of traumatic experiences linked to bullying. Through the process of sharing her story, she commented that she found narrating these earlier episodes 'quite tiring'. It was through the recollection of these experiences that Alyce became emotional, as she described the death of a close teenage friend: 'I'm crying – I never cry, not even when my parents passed away' and that she 'got so emotional thinking about him'. She states this was the first time she had recalled this memory to another person:

> High school was the worst for me. The first week, I was assaulted by several older boys at the train station on the way home. I was pushed to the ground, held down, and two or three of them had lipstick that they used to write on my face. One used it to make up my lips. Everyone on the train station laughed at me. When I got home, my mother cleaned my face before I saw what they wrote. She went to the school to complain, but the Brothers wrote it off as nothing more than hazing.

> My other major problem was P.E. (gym class). We had to shower after the class, and being naked in front of the other boys was torture to me. I was ridiculed endlessly. I did anything possible to avoid gym.

Alyce said that she had got so emotional in recounting these adolescent years because she was thinking about the only good friend she had at high school: 'He got me through High School with as little harassment as possible.' Alyce's friend died in a hunting accident in 1989, which is why telling the story was emotionally charged for her:

He protected me. I was picked on all the time, but never when he was around. He told me to stop wearing tight shirts that emphasized my breasts. He pointed out that I sometimes let my wrist go limp, or that I should learn to speak in a lower register because my natural voice was high and 'squeaky'.

Alyce explains how her and Jerry's childhood experiences were 'rough'. She tells how Jerry was beaten up daily by other boys. He had to visit a paediatrician who gave him medication to calm his nerves at this time. It was also a solitary suffering, as Jerry 'had no one to turn to'. Alyce describes their teenage development and anxiety as an 'evil mentality' and Jerry 'was petrified to tell anyone how he felt'.

Alyce's experiences of shame are contrastable with those of Poppy, one of Cornwall's participants. Poppy states:

The Catholic Church just seems much more accepting and much more open. And to be much more, actually, about the mercy and the love of God, and forgiveness and hope. Some people I say that to think it's a little bit funny, because I think their perception is it's all about guilt and shame and judgment. I haven't really found that. (Cornwall, 2014, p. 224)

There are a wide range of variables by which both Poppy and Alyce's experiences could be compared and contrasted. It could be surmised that Poppy's age is significantly lower than Alyce's, thus representing a childhood which is contextually located in an age of more liberal politics, sexual freedom and tolerance towards individuals. That said, Cornwall does state that her ten participants are aged between early thirties and late sixties, so Poppy could be of similar age to Alyce. The settings of the USA (Alyce) and UK (Poppy) could also be significant. Nevertheless, individualized life stories and accounts are subjective and should not be treated as universal truths.

It is therefore important to remember that a single experience cannot speak for all intersex experiences. Iain Morland reminds us that there is a 'narrative plurality' (2009, p. 194) when looking at lives and experiences of those who identify as intersex, and that 'there may be more than one narrative about intersex, and those narratives may differ radically' (2009, p. 196). Cornwall also acknowledges this plurality of stories as she states that 'the voices narrating intersex/DSD are always multiple, that there is no such thing as monolithic intersex/DSD experience' (2010a, p. 224). She continues that 'engaging with polyphonic narratives means engaging with this tension, the "queerness" of what may appear to be a lack of cohesion or consensus in intersex/DSD history' (2010a, p. 224).

Although Morland and Cornwall both discuss the multiplicity of voices narrating intersex experiences, they are talking across a range of individuals, concluding that there is no consentient intersex experience. Within Alyce/Jerry's narrative, the emphasis on the polyphonic nature of intersex bodies becomes even more nuanced as I note the plurality of voices, narratives and experience within one embodiment.

This shame experienced during the youthful years seems to emerge from Jerry/Alyce's own parents' attitudes towards gender and sexual physicality. In recounting a childhood experience, Alyce notes:

My mother never let me go to the men's room by myself. If we were out and my father wasn't around, she would take me to the ladies' room.

I couldn't talk to my parents, they had the Puritan/Catholic attitude that sex was evil outside the context of marriage. And even then, it was only for procreation. The funny thing about it was that it was never about sex. It was gender; I didn't want to have sex with anyone. I just wanted to feel comfortable with my identity.

One day, I came home from school to find my secret stash of women's clothes thrown on my bed. They were some of my mother's old clothes she wouldn't miss that I commandeered. I had been found out, and I was terrified. I ran out of the house, hoping to avoid confrontation. But that was only a temporary fix, I had to go back home sometime. I stayed out as long as I could, and when I got home, I was greeted with a stern, disapproving look from my mother. She then scolded me for being late for dinner.

Although never discussed, there was a powerful silence which reigned over those issues. Alyce comments:

> That was it, no mention of the clothes. And when I went back to my room, they were gone. I never saw them again, and nothing was ever mentioned about them. I can imagine them concluding that it was just a phase I was going through, and that I'd grow out of it. Truth is, they were probably more frightened to discuss the matter than I was.

Despite the recognition that the parents of Alyce/Jerry were afraid to discuss the matter of gender presentation, this powerful silencing is a shaming strategy. Within the literature on practical theology, Stephen Pattison's extensive work on shaming within Christianity rightfully exposes shame as an area of theological enquiry which has not received as much attention as guilt. He notes how the nude body, as an expression of sexuality, has been a site of shame in Christianity since the incident between Adam and Eve (Pattison, 2000, p. 267). Although Pattison does not deal with intersex bodies directly, he does observe the following:

> Notoriously, Christianity has been particularly harsh in its attitudes towards gay people and other embodied 'sexual deviants' (amongst whom one could number the whole of womankind!) ... The implied, non-specific condemnation of all things bodily and sexual must therefore do much to increase fundamental shame amongst young people who are exposed to Christian morality. (2000, p. 267)

Alyce's religious upbringing therefore contributes to the shaming. Shame is equally illustrated in the discussions of Jerry and Alyce's physicality:

> He wants a bigger penis, I wish it was gone. He's ashamed of his

breasts, I want bigger breasts.

But I knew from a very early age that I wanted to be a woman. Long before my breasts developed. Although this is probably considered medically inaccurate, I feel like I'm XX and the Y is the errant chromosome. I would have preferred treatment with female hormones and removal of the offending appendage.

The similarities between Alyce's narrative and stories of gender transition struck me throughout the interviews. Stephen Craig Kerry argues for clear distinctions to be made between transgender and intersex identities, noting how some intersex individuals may be transgender, but that transgender individuals are not necessarily intersex:

It is essential, first, to emphasize that transgender is not synonymous with intersex; indeed the intersex movement has made it quite clear that transgenderism and intersex are not the same thing. Yet some intersex individuals, assigned and raised one sex/gender, identify as the other in adulthood. Whilst transgender people are not intersex, some intersex individuals are transgender; that is, dissatisfied with the medically determined sex/gender, they have reassigned themselves to their true sex/gender. (2015, p. 133)

In terms of transitioning or considering gender-reassignment surgery, Alyce questioned whether such procedures could potentially be a rejection of God's creation:

I am not considering transitioning. That should have been four decades ago. It would take a few years, money I don't have, I'd risk losing my family, and I'd end up being a woman in her mid-sixties with no memories.

Here's what I'm aiming for, a more androgynous appearance. I'm losing weight, I'm grooming myself (I considered good grooming to be feminine and made a point to be sloppy in all respects), and in general, stop trying to be more masculine than I am.

A final point about how I feel about sin and religion. If the 1960s were more like today, I am pretty sure I would have transitioned. Not for sexual reasons, but rather to align my body with my mind. But I'm not sure that would have been the right thing to do. Would that be a rejection of the person God made me? Would I, in essence, be blaming God for being a freak? Could God make such a mistake, and would I be arrogant thinking man/science could fix it? Or, did I commit a sin by not living the life God intended for me? I lived someone else's life by conforming to society's norms. Maybe that's the greater sin.

The conflict between body and mind is at the core of Jerry and Alyce's duality. In this next section, I explore the duel of dual experiences, the dominance of Jerry and the resentment Alyce has felt to Jerry.

Performing Gender: The Duel of Duality

The first thing that needs to be said is that neither Jerry nor I can ever really be happy with our body. Even if you get past the major male genitalia/breast issue, every part of us is unsatisfactory to both of us. Let's take my hand for example. I think it's not feminine enough, he thinks the fingers are too long and slender for a man. It's like everything's a compromise, and that's the best either of us can hope for. Something neither this nor that.

Alyce described Jerry's body as 'hideous'. Alyce and Jerry's gendered subjectivities are both real and discursively constructed. Although Alyce and Jerry cannot be decoupled in any bodily form, Alyce acknowledges that Jerry is the dominant persona physically, whereas Alyce exists mostly 'in mind only', and this is detailed further in the later discussion of sex. The 'neither this nor that' third option which Alyce articulates is one which is later explored as Alyce describes how the Trinity serves as a useful explanation for intersex bodies which are dissatisfied with the either/or binary of male/female. Indeed, this 'neither this nor that' feeling is one which resulted in a constant struggle between Jerry and Alyce.

First, the duel of duality was most highlighted in a physical form when it came to weight:

> We hadn't quite recognized our duality, but still there was a constant struggle between me and him. And you could tell who was winning by weight. I wanted to be thin, he was content being heavy. In his mind, thin made him look more feminine. He would get to a certain weight (about 155 lbs), and then start binge eating because he thought he was getting 'too thin'. Once, I actually managed to get all the way down to 140 lbs, and I looked good when I had the opportunity to fix myself up. One night, I fought off his urges and actually went outside. It was cold, and there was snow on the ground. I even drove my car around the block, but returned after a few minutes because I only had ID in Jerry's name. I enjoyed feeling the cold wind blow under my dress, it wasn't nearly as bad as I imagined it would be. Walking in ice and snow was a little tricky in heels, but I managed (walking in heels came naturally to me from the beginning). I was in heaven, and felt like I wanted so much more, but the next day Jerry started binge eating again.

This is the first and only occasion Alyce narrates going out and presenting as Alyce. She explores the possibility of making Alyce real in physical terms, by seeking to adopt a more androgynous look, and in this way accepting the body God gave her:

> The more I do this (interacting as Alyce on social network sites), the stronger my desire is to make Alyce real in the physical sense. It's no longer enough for me to exist in mind only, I want to interact with people in person. Not full time, I'd like to find a balance where I can live the life I have, but also be Alyce when I want. That's why I view an androgynous look to be the only realist way of finding the balance I seek. In a way, it almost seems that I would be accepting the body God gave me instead of fighting it like I have for all my life. Is it realistic? I don't know, but it does seem to be the only possibility that makes any sense to me.

This notion of Alyce in 'mind' becomes more apparent as she

discusses how she now dreams as Alyce. She also comments that the voice she hears in her head when she writes as Alyce is markedly more feminized that Jerry's voice. This contrasts sharply with the unpleasant dreams Jerry had where he was presenting as a female in public, as she continues:

> I am now Alyce when I dream. I don't see myself, but I always interact with the people in my dreams as Alyce, and that's how they see me. I had always wanted to be a woman in my dreams, even read about controlling your thoughts before sleep to influence what you dream about, but it never happened. There were a lot of dreams about Jerry being in public dressed in woman's clothing, but those dreams were always unpleasant.

The duel of duality between Alyce and Jerry resulted in her describing them as a 'freak'. In offering a positive reconciliation between their appearance, Alyce discussed how true acceptance would be through the wearing of male and female swimming garments, and, although she dismisses this as 'ridiculous' the 'neither this nor that' current embodiment results in a reduced sense of modesty and embarrassment:

> This might seem odd, but in my mind true acceptance would be going outside to our pool (we live in an apartment complex with a public pool) wearing male swim trunks and a bikini top. I know it's ridiculous and not at all practical, but so is swimming bare breasted. Not only is it embarrassing, but it violates my sense of modesty.

While exploring her gender presentation as Alyce has been complex in a physical sense, the internet has been the place where Alyce has found a space in which to express and explore herself.

Online Gender Trouble

Kate O'Riordan and Heather White explored queer spiritual practices online, looking at virtual believers. Their case study discussed how the combinations of identities: queer, spiritual, and digital, created 'a freedom from the constraints of heteronormativity, homonormativity, religious dogma, and sometimes life in the "real"' (O'Riordan and White, 2010, p. 230). Thriving communities that identify as non-normative or queer can be found online, whereas in pre-internet times such groups were difficult to reach. Kessler agrees, 'members of the gay, lesbian, bi, trans (GLBT) community, for example, ... need only jump online to find thriving communities that self-identify as queer' (2011, p. 125).

Before domestic and work-based usage of the internet in the UK became more widespread, Shelley Correll's US-based study of an electronic lesbian café reflects the popularity of internet usage with gay and lesbian communities. She states that online anonymity is what attracts the online users 'to try out a behaviour that they consider to be deviant' (Correll, 1995, p. 271). The significance of cyberspace as a more inclusive area than heteronormative society makes it a popular choice for those who feel on the margins of mainstream society because of their sexual exoticism. Saskia Sassen and Chris Ashford agree with the liberating nature of the internet:

Individuals and groups which have historically been excluded ... can find in cyberspace an enabling environment both for their emergence as non-formal political actors and for their struggles. (Sassen, 2002, p. 382)

Sexual minority groups, and/or those groups deemed sexually deviant, limited by the constraints of space, are able to interact through virtual media. (Ashford, 2009, p. 299)

The internet thus provides a more accessible space. It offers the possibility of a non-heteronormative, non-hegemonic, liminal space, yet this does not negate the increasing concerns of the internet being a place where bullying and harassment can take place, which is widely documented due to incidents occurring on social media. The internet as a space has changed since its initial growth in the 1990s. Ashford views this as a positive liberation: 'cyberspace, freeing us from corporeal bounds, enables a queering of the self' (2009, p. 299). It is within digital spaces that gender and sexuality are not always presumed:

> The virtual world has provided new opportunities for sexual connections, interactions and communities to emerge. It enables people to try out new sexual identities unrestricted by the limitations of their real bodies. (Johnston and Longhurst, 2010, p. 3)

Understanding identity in the digital age is a complex process. Sherry Turkle has been pioneering in researching concepts of online identity presentations, and her significant text, *Life on the Screen* (1995), explores how digital media enables individuals to generate their own online identities. An online presence permits multiple identity negotiations, as Turkle states:

> The Internet has become a significant social laboratory for experimenting with the constructions and reconstructions of self that characterise postmodern life. In its virtual reality, we self-fashion and self-create. (1995, p. 180)

Such self-fashioned and self-created personas signify that presenting oneself on screen makes it much easier to present oneself differently to who/how one is in real life. Turkle's text includes a significant contribution which relates to presenting oneself as the other gender, which she calls 'virtual gender swapping' (1995, p. 212) and engaging in sexual activities, in her section 'virtual sex' (1995, p. 223). Although this gender-play can be interpreted as a harmless experience, we must remember that the internet is not an insignificant playground in which to experiment. Turkle stresses the space of internet experimentation as 'psychologically challenging … that is not without some grave and emotional risk' (1995, p. 213).

Robert Kitchin describes the online arena as a space of deviancy: 'cyberspace is creating a new space of deviancy, a space that provides a social context where the socially alienated can occupy and play out their fantasies' (1998, pp. 400–01). The use of the internet can serve as a freeing and liberating place, thus enabling participants to be more honest when articulating secret behaviours and practices:

Many people feel inhibited by their embodied selves, but

(disembodied) personal homepages allow them to speak more authentically and in words and ways that they might not in their offline lives. Moreover, personal homepages are different from other documents because they are living; that is, they are up-to-date and modifiable. (Stern, 2003, p. 257)

Because of the relative anonymity of Internet communication settings, ... we argue that one's true self is more likely to be active during Internet than face-to-face interactions. (Bargh et al. 2002, p. 44)

Alyce's existence online far outweighs her existence in reality. Her online activity is not one of gender-swapping; rather it allows her to express her personality, which does not match her quotidian bodily presentation. Yet within this online interaction, feelings of guilt and deception lurk. Equally, the duel of duality between Jerry and Alyce was played out behind the screen, as Alyce notes:

I would love to talk about cyber Alyce. Jerry was apprehensive at first, he was certain that everyone would immediately know that I was him. He wouldn't even let me befriend him on Facebook, he was afraid someone he knew would link us together.

After gaining in confidence online ... Even Jerry befriended me (on Facebook)!

You don't really think about it, but the ads that pop up on my Facebook are totally different than Jerry's ads. He gets guitar stores, I get shoes and clothing. I spend way too much of my time picking out my anticipated wardrobe.

Identities formulated through the internet are often carefully considered and constructed, before they are published in the form of a profile. Susannah Stern notes, 'one does not exist in cyberspace until one literally writes oneself into existence' (2003, p. 256). The internet therefore provides a tool in which biographies are created. Such background self-presentation work in constructing one's profile does not always mean a person is being deceptive.

Indeed, Jenny Davis effectively reminds us that behind-the-scenes work exists in offline contexts too, 'similar backstage work goes on prior to interaction in offline spaces as well (e.g. the woman who meticulously plans the exact outfit and hairstyle she will wear to a job interview)' (2010, p. 1114).

Alyce has written her own history. She notes how her birth was selected when she created her Facebook profile, it is 'not the day we were actually born, but the day I chose for my Facebook profile'. She bases her social interactions on a need for expression and interaction with others:

> I'm on Facebook and Google+ and having a great time interacting with other people as the woman Alyce. But I've created my own history, and one of the major differences is that Alyce is 20 years younger than Jerry.

> I *need* [her emphasis] to interact with others as Alyce, that's the reason for the social media. The profile is made up, but there is an element of truth in most of it. I am 20 years younger, but that was to better match the only two pictures of my face in makeup. The guilt? I am a Catholic girl, after all.

For Alyce, the internet is the place 'to explore conflicts raised by one's biological gender' (Turkle, 1995, p. 213). Both Alyce and Jerry identify as Christian online, but Alyce notes how 'Jerry's beliefs are a lot more conservative'. The guilt Alyce expresses is rooted in her feelings of deception in presenting herself as 'other' than she is in real life (Jerry), although she turns to social media with the intention of exploring and releasing Alyce. Rather than a deceptive act, her portrayal of Alyce on social media provides an alternate space in which the boundary between the real and the desired can play out and coexist: her body no longer imprisons her mind. Lövheim and Linderman are aware of the possibilities of the 'body-less context of the internet' yet remind us that 'identity constructions still seem to be a social process – a process in relation to other individuals' (2005, p. 121). This communication of one's identity as a social process is one which Slevin explored in his work on the internet and society (2000). The internet allows an individual to engage in a project of creating a meaningful and integrated self-identity which is communicated without the bodily restraints of the physical form. In physical terms, Alyce's narration of both her and Jerry's sexual stories explores the intersections across the themes of duality and gender complexities. The duality of these complexities is highlighted in the frank discussion of both Alyce and Jerry's sex lives, to which attention now turns.

Intersex, Into Sex

Alyce proved to be open and frank about sex, with reference to both her and Jerry's sex lives. She initially protested saying she minded speaking about the theme, but then stated, 'only teasing'. Her first discussion took the form of describing Jerry's sex life:

> For the first thirty years, there was no sex with anyone. Jerry desired several women, but could never allow it to reach a level of intimacy because he was ashamed of his body. Jerry is easy to define. He's a heterosexual male. He goes out of his way to project a manly image, does not want to appear gay or fem in any way. He has never felt attraction to any male.

Jerry lost his virginity as the age of 29, and despite concerns about the size of his penis and ability to perform, Alyce comments how his first sexual partner 'never complained about the size of his penis, but complimented him for being an attentive lover'. This comment was also reiterated when Alyce mentions Jerry's first sexual encounter with his current wife, who has the pseudonym Kirsty. Alyce summarizes Jerry's sex life in three words 'just two women'. Alyce explains how Jerry's sex life with his wife is no longer existent. She shares a memory recalling the evening before Jerry married, he destroyed all traces of Alyce in a fire, and she ceased to exist for a short while. During the marriage, Jerry fathered two daughters, as Alyce details:

> PS – Maybe something I should mention. Jerry never thought he could father children, but he was wrong about that. But the fact that they were able to have two was a blessing, but they

should have had many more. He wasn't sterile, but I think he did have a low sperm count because they tried hard to have a child right away but it took a couple of years. But here's the point: at first, Jerry didn't worry about protection because he thought he couldn't father children. But Kirsty became pregnant in the year preceding the wedding. She wanted to abort, but he was dead set against it. He refused to pay for it, but he did take her to the clinic and took care of her afterwards. He explained that he wouldn't pay for it because it was a sin against his religion. It ripped apart his soul, and he drank heavily for several weeks. He still regrets that he wasn't stronger and that he should have convinced her to keep the baby. He raised his two daughters on Christian values, love, peace, tolerance, but he never took them to Church. I hold those same values, so I like to think I also had some hand in raising them as well.

A similar observation in relation to the fathering of children being a perceived determinant of gender is made by Martha Coventry, who was met with matter-of-fact responses by her father and doctor when she began to explore and question her gender identity: 'My father and my doctor had the same sensible response when I asked what sex I really was: "You had children, isn't that proof enough?"' Martha's response was simply 'No, as a matter of fact, it wasn't' (Coventry, 1999, p. 72).

Alyce's claim to involvement in the raising of Jerry's daughters is expressed poignantly, and for the first time, there is a commonality to the essences of Jerry and Alyce regarding the Catholic values both hold. The story of the abortion, alongside the expression of regret on Jerry's behalf, is narrated with an adherence to traditional Catholic values.

After considering Jerry's sex life, Alyce moved on to describe her own. There is a constraint she has in describing her own sex life, as sex is commonly understood in physical terms. Alyce's sexual gratification is often in her mind, largely experienced through episodes of dressing up. Ultimately, she finds fulfilment in being able to embody Alyce's appearance:

Alyce is more cerebral than physical. She describes herself as asexual, but it's more complicated than that. Like Jerry, she's attracted to feminine beauty. But it's more envy than lust. She does not find men attractive, but she does fantasize about having a nondescript male make love to her. She wants to be a woman and experience everything about being a physical woman. Jerry sees a woman and finds her attractive. Alyce sees her and wants to be her.

Alyce adds an interesting addendum to this by stating: '(I don't want to get too analytical, but maybe I want to be her because I know HE finds her attractive?)'. This, of course, raises questions which psychoanalysts could ponder: Does Alyce seek to please Jerry? Or is Jerry the only male who knows about her and so she seeks his masculine approval?

Alyce describes herself as 'asexual' because of the lack of female sex organs, as she says:

> I think I consider myself asexual because I don't have the proper sex organs. I just don't feel any desire there. What's there is his, and I really don't want any part of it. Well, that's not entirely true. In fantasy, I will play with it but it's not part of me. It's as if I am playing with his (or someone's) penis. It's totally detached from me.

Asexuality has been largely overlooked to date, and remains unreferenced in the indexes of many publications that claim to discuss queer or sexual theology. In my view, sexual and queer theology should encompass asexuality. Asexuality is radical because both society and religion expects sexual relationality. Elizabeth Stuart comments:

> Asexual people are currently an almost completely silenced group within the theology of sexuality ... and the asexual person should raise uncomfortable questions for all of us who have valorised sex and sexual desire perhaps at the expense of relationship. Have we in the process aided the alienation of our asexual brothers and sisters and placed them out of the economy of salvation? (2014, p. 29)

Jerry certainly is dominant when it comes to an expression of

Alyce's sexuality, which is detailed in the section below:

> But no matter how many hours Alyce spent fixing herself up, doing her hair (wig), nails, makeup, removing unwanted hair, Jerry could always end it. She would stare at the finished product in the mirror, evaluating herself ... Then he would take over and masturbate to her image, and that would end Alyce for time being. What took her hours to create, he would make vanish in minutes.

What is significant about this quotation from Alyce is how she refers to herself in the third person. This slip of accuracy is one which did not go unnoticed for Alyce, who in a follow up email commented: 'I'm sorry I repeated myself in the last email, I had it saved in DRAFTS and didn't realize I had already sent it (although I had changed it from 3rd person to first).' Alyce then modified and resent the email (my emphasis):

> But no matter how many hours *I* spent fixing *myself* up, doing *my* hair (wig), nails, makeup, removing unwanted hair, Jerry could always end it. *I* would stare at the finished product in the mirror, evaluating myself... Then he would take over and masturbate to *my* image, and that would end *me* for time being. What took *me* hours to create, he would make vanish in minutes. When he was done, *I* was done. He couldn't wait to remove all traces of *me*.

Alyce commented on her cautious use of language: 'I'm very careful with words.' This care and attention given to producing her life story with clarity and accuracy serves to ensure a distinct clarity between the complex embodiment of Jerry and Alyce. Her narrative is restricted by her own adherence to the use of male or female pronouns. Significantly, this slippage in pronouns discussed above was not one in which Jerry became the narrator, indeed both Jerry and Alyce are referred to in the third person, as if it were written by another party. If we look at the first narration, both Jerry and Alyce are brought into being through the use of the third person singular. In the second text, Alyce uses the first person singular.

To return briefly to the account of Jerry 'taking over' from Alyce's self-creation and dominating the space through his masturbation, it becomes apparent that Alyce is unwillingly subversive to Jerry's dominance. His destruction of her intimate space is an assault on her gender performativity. In an extended discussion of her own sex life since 2010, Alyce again describes how Jerry's penis is implied in all her sexual encounters, offering her the sensation of orgasm, yet Alyce starts to take control of the sexualized space. The result in the pleasuring of both Jerry and Alyce is one which has been negotiated to result in mutual pleasure:

Here's how my sex life has been since about 2010. I would dress (but never do my face), typically bra, panties, stockings, full slip, and heels. If I knew I had time, I would put a dress on and just be myself for a while. There was one week where everyone went back East to visit Kirsty's family while I stayed home, I was probably dressed up for 1/4 of the time. The difference now was that I was starting to separate myself into male and female personalities. And Jerry no longer controlled the situation all the time, I started taking control. And when I did it, it was amazing.

Since I lacked the necessary female parts, my erogenous zones were my breasts. Specifically my nipples which would harden as I played with them. I would soon lose myself in fantasy, imagining myself being a total woman being made love to. Always eyes closed. I had no image of a specific male, just the sensation that one was there behind me, reaching around and playing with my breasts. Hugging me tight. I was, in that moment, just me. No thought of Jerry, nor was there anything remotely male about me. Eventually I would sense the penis, but again it felt detached from me. I would start to play with it with one hand, while he continued playing with my breast with the other. It's strange, but it was like two different people servicing each other. And when it was at its best, we both climaxed. To explain, there would naturally be the expected male ejaculation and all that implies. But then I would also feel something within my groin, like a quivering sensation. Often I would be standing in my heels doing this, and I would sometimes lose my balance because the feeling was so intense. Also, unlike earlier times, there was no urgent need for me to get immediately out of my clothes. I could linger about and savor the moment, and often it would take a minute or two to fully return to reality. I would even continue to lightly play with my breast, not to re-arouse myself, but rather keep me in the moment as long as possible.

The sexual narrative offered above is one which serves to increase awareness of the complex nature of gender and the relationship Alyce has with Jerry, both contained within the same flesh and skin. This relationship is expressed by Alyce in theological terms, using the Trinity as a metaphor for the understanding and acceptance of their identities. The internet and the Trinity both create the ideal settings for a theology of intersex to be communicated.

The Intersex Tranity

The wordplay here does not seek to produce an alternative theological lexicon to discuss the Trinity, but rather it reflects the nature of transgression which is a theme in how intersex individuals posit themselves as made in the image of God. *Trans-* does not signify transsexual or transgendered which are both personable categories of identification. *Trans-* here comes from the term transgression and transformation.

Elizabeth Stuart has claimed that 'we are all part of the Trinity' (1995, p. 244), noting how the 'problem that many of us have with the Trinity is that it seems to portray God as self-sufficient' (1995, p. 243). Utilizing the Christian understanding of the church as the body of Christ on earth, Althaus-Reid develops this further, allowing for the displacement of sexual theological knowledge:

> This would mean that all these suppressed, displaced embodiments of knowledge could feel at home in the Trinity, just as the Trinity should feel at home in gay bars and S/M scenes, displacing temporary hegemonies and allowing a real plurality of religious experiences and theological practices. (2003a, p. 75)

Alyce's theology is one which locates herself, Jerry and the possibility of a 'third person' that could reconcile the duel between Jerry and Alyce. This 'third person' provides an option for satisfaction, which neither Jerry nor Alyce feel they can achieve. For Alyce, this 'third person' would be 'androgynous' in terms of the performed gender. Alyce states:

> There is one God, but He's comprised of three distinct entities. They are all God, but they're not the same being. The Father is not the Son who's not the Holy Spirit who's not the Father ... One is not more powerful than the others, they're all the same even though they're not the same.

> If I decided to split my life between Alyce and Jerry, people would see two entirely different people. If I adopted an androgynous persona, it could be a totally different third person. I could be any one of those three personas, but I'd still be Me. It would be just how I decide to manifest myself. I don't know if that's good analogy, but it kind of makes sense to me.

Thus, thinking of intersex bodies as three rather than two opens up possibilities for gender satisfaction, and a resolution to the 'neither this nor that' identity which has been part of Alyce and Jerry's histories.

In her work on a feminist reading of the Trinity, Hannah Bacon (2009) suggests a shift from the traditional focus on God to a more inclusive understanding of the Trinity. Her critique is of the language used to speak about the Trinity, which is traditionally androcentric and male (God the Father, God the Son). Bacon therefore exposes how language limits our construct of God. Feminist theology has sought to de-sex and depersonalize the Trinity from its traditional male presumptions.[3] For Bacon, the Trinity means expanse. It needs to be expansive enough for ambiguities and multiplicities. In such terms, an expansive Trinity defies a monological view of God, and if it is to be useful to feminist theology, it must be able to celebrate diverse, multiple and ambiguous embodiments.

In order to understand how the Trinity can be more expansive, Bacon developed the notion of thinking 'back' from incarnation to the Trinity, as 'the triune God cannot be God without the flesh'

(2012, p. 443). Reading back from the incarnation specifically means we must be conscious of our own embodied selves. The Trinity is thus exposed to be fleshy rather than rigid, speculative abstraction, and Bacon highlights how the fleshiness of the Trinity serves to alleviate feminist concerns in relation to Christologies. As traditional Christology has been unable to conceive God's identity other than through the (male) body of Christ, reading back from our own embodied selves allows the ambiguities of gender and sexuality to be reflected in the Trinity. God therefore moves to being more expansive rather than one-dimensional: 'Thinking God as Trinity ... provides a theological resource for thinking about intersectionality and for affirming the fluidities and ambiguities of identity' (Bacon, 2012, p. 443).

The Trinity certainly offers a 'third space' or a liminal space, which allows us to deconstruct, in theological terms, the boundaries that define our gendered identities. Queering gender identity through a troubling of fixed boundaries is exactly how Alyce/Jerry see themselves and more specifically, how they see themselves in the image of God. Bacon's affirmation that 'The Trinity ... exposes that God is ambiguous and diverse ... and that bodies are not "other" to what God is' (2012, p. 456) serves to release gender and sex from binary positions, and thus allow other non-normative individuals to connect meaningfully to God. A similar discussion here comes from Gerard Loughlin (2004) who reminds us that the Trinity is a figurative metaphor and that creation echoes the Trinity: 'We can see creation is properly a parody of the Trinity, a non-identical repetition in the order of created being of the trinitarian relations, which are now seen to be determinative of human bodies, but not of human sexes' (Loughlin, 2004, p. 156).

Furthermore, Althaus-Reid attempts to conceptualize a Trinity beyond numerology (2000b, p. 220), which would 'provide us with a better God-in-community pattern than trying to include the ubiquitous female presence to fit between the Father and the Son' (2000b, p. 220). Given the unlikelihood that a higher numerical model could replace the notion of three within the grand narrative of the Trinity, it is useful to think of the Trinity as including both male and female, rather than relying just on the language of the masculine relations. Bacon calls for a 'generous' theology when thinking about the Trinity, one 'which does not limit women or men to static, predefined, designated symbolic material, or social spaces' (2012, p. 442). She continues:

> Thinking about God must be generous in its imaginings so that it allows for the fluidities, multiplicities, ambiguities, complexities and the diversities of women and men's embodiments to be theologically theorized, valued and embraced. (2012, p. 442)

Nonetheless, Sarah Coakley observes that although orthodox Christianity claims that God is beyond gender, theologians cannot escape the cultural and historical assumptions about the Trinity and the language used to discuss Father and Son:

> There can be little doubt ... of the prevailing paradox in classic Christianity: the persistent orthodox refrain that God, qua God, is beyond gender; and the equally persistent appearance of gendered visual representations of that God, often in forms which vividly display cultural assumptions about 'normative' gender roles. (2013, p. 248)

If the Trinity allows for the diversity of men and women's embodiments to be valued, we must remember that we are talking about a Godhead which is both male and female. Cornwall agrees that it is this notion of 'both male and female' rather than Alyce's description of 'neither this nor that' that supports a God made in our image:

> the representation of the Trinity – must be both male and female (still based in a binary paradigm, grounded in lack-and-completion) rather than beyond male and female. To suppose that (human) sex attributes tell the whole truth of God is to settle for a God made in our image without adequately examining why our self-identification is as it is in the first place. (Cornwall, 2010a, p. 106)

Coakley discusses how Gregory of Nyssa sought to transcend gender. For Gregory, she argues, gender is a secondary feature of human existence, and although it is of bodily import, it is the soul which displaces the body; it is through the soul that we reflect God:

> The message Gregory evidently wishes to convey is that gender stereotypes must be reversed, undermined, and transcended if the soul is to advance to supreme intimacy with the Trinitarian God, and that the language of sexuality and gender, far from being an optional aside or mere rhetorical flourish in the process, is somehow necessary and intrinsic to the epistemological deepening that Gregory seeks to describe. (Coakley, 2002, p. 128)

If queer theology seeks to 'outwit identity' (Loughlin, 2008, p. 149), then an intersex reflection on the Tranity seeks to outwit genitalia. Thus a theology of the Tranity does not begin from the viewpoint of male or female, 'neither this nor that', but it encompasses both male and female yet relegates the import of bodily appendages such as genitalia, in favour of prioritizing the soul as a vessel of God. This does not render all humans genderless and sexless; rather, it prioritizes the personhood over genitalia. Cornwall summarizes this point appropriately, 'God by definition breaks out of human model' (2010a, p. 214). For Alyce, thinking about God's gender is one which must ultimately result in acceptance:

> As far as God's gender, I was taught that I was made in His image and likeness. Therefore, God is just like me. Of course, everyone can make the same claim. But the bottom line is that God made me as I am, and I must accept that and thank Him. I'm working on it.

Alyce considers herself inherently spiritual, expressing the desire to be baptized:

> I have no doubt that God's Spirit still lives in my soul, and His Spirit is there to guide me. He made me, He loves me, and He wants me to find peace and happiness. He certainly doesn't want me to be unhappy. I think I would like to be baptized as Alyce.

Within the Tranity, the relationship of *perichoresis* is useful, as the notion of 'indwelling' helps to problematize theologically the fixedness of gender and sexuality. This serves to counter a tradition that has historically ascribed certain actions to each divine person, and tried almost to define and thereby limit the intersections between Father, Son and Spirit. Acknowledging that each dwells in the others, we can employ the metaphor of a dance within the Trinity, so that the fluidness and transience of the divine persons comes much more to the fore.

Alyce's strong faith is expressed in her views of God, the Trinity and upholding Christian values. In addition to sharing her story with me, Alyce also produced some literature, which expresses the ideas of her faith.

Creative Creeds

In Chapter 2, I noted how Judith Halberstam reminded us of the importance of taking detours and using mixed media to engage with creative queer research. Alyce offered a short story that she wrote. She comments, 'Alyce is a major character in the story, it's almost like I'm creating my own history. I'm beginning to feel like a real person'. In theological terms, there is an abiding profundity of the story, which is one which notices the ultimate triumph of God's radical and extravagant acceptance.

Robert Graham observes, 'the untruth of fiction may be more powerful and more significant than truth' (1989, p. 101), and although Alyce's narrative is partially created through fictional events, the truth lies in how Alyce uses them to form her biography and reclaim 'lost years' through Jerry's dominance.

A Glorious Day

It was a glorious Sunday morning. The heat spell had broken, and the oppressive humidity had surrendered to a cool, gentle breeze blowing steadily from the coast. And with that ocean breeze came a sense of rejuvenation, maybe even rebirth, and for the first time in a long time I felt like I had a future of my own.

The westerly wind pushed aside the gray gloom and restored the blue skies of brighter times. The dark clouds, always threatening to erupt with the crack of Satan's whip, gave way to God's billows of pure, angelic white.

I opened my bedroom window so that I might inhale the miracle of this magnificent morn. And even though I lived ninety miles inland, I could still hear the ocean roar, feel the morning mist upon my face, and taste its saline waters upon my lips and tongue.

But still, I yearned for so much more. Something undefined, yet something so tangible I could feel it in my spirit, mind and body. A force so powerful that it can tear me into a thousand pieces without destroying the sheer and delicate fabric of my soul. A force so forgiving that it could pardon all my sins, real and imaginary. A force so loving that it can accept me, imperfect as I am.

There's a park near my apartment; I walked past it every day on my way home from work. I never gave it much thought, never took the time to enjoy the serenity it offered, I was always too anxious to get home and 'relax'. This morning seemed to be the perfect time to explore this small patch of nature nestled away in the midst of endless miles of concrete.

I was instantly intoxicated by the fragrance of the flowers, mingled with the sweet aroma of the Acacia trees which adorned the pathway through the park. It was dizzying; I felt as if my spirit broke free of the bondage of flesh and blood, free to walk the path without touching the ground, free of trivial matters that consume our human existence.

I heard music in the distance. So faint that my ears could not distinguish it, but yet so compelling that my soul could sense its very essence and know it was heavenly. Could it be a hallucination, brought on by nature's perfumed intoxicant? No, it was real, and it was calling out to me. And I was irresistibly drawn to it.

I walked in the direction of the music, passing by the house that my husband and I used to live in. It still looked the same, but at the same time, it was very different. Children were playing on the front lawn, young children maybe seven or eight years old, enjoying life as only children can.

By this time, I realized the source of the music. It was coming from the nearby Catholic Church, Our Lady of Solitude. It was our parish when we lived in that house. It was where we were married.

I recognized the music; the church was celebrating a high mass. Pipe organ. Choir. Gregorian chant. Majestic and absolutely beautiful. I remember going to high mass when I was a young girl, 10:00 A.M. every Sunday morning. Now they have guitars and singers singing modern music. It's just not the same.

I approached the church, anxious to join in the celebration. But as I reached the front doors, I was overcome with the feeling that I was no longer welcomed. I felt like an outcast, someone that did not belong there anymore.

I decided to remain outside. After all, it was a gorgeous day.

Behind the church, there was a dirt path lined with the Stations of the Cross. By each station, a stone bench barely wide enough to fit two people. I sat down by the sixth station, and listened to the music coming from the church.

I was so lost in the splendor of the moment, I didn't even notice the man standing next to my bench. He asked if he might join me.

There were plenty of empty benches, why did he want to squeeze in with me? I was going to tell him to get his own bench when I looked up and discovered he was a priest.

'Of course, Father,' I answered, scooting over to make room for him. I was familiar with his calf length cassock, which I recognized from my college days, and asked if he was a member of the Society.

'Ad Maiorem Dei Gloriam,' he replied.

'For the greater glory of God,' I repeated.

I started to introduce myself, but he abruptly stopped me before I could tell him my name. He cocked his head and looked at me, as if he were critiquing a painting.

'Your name is … Veronica,' he said with complete assurance. I shook my head no.

'Magdalena?'

'No!' I chuckled.

The priest shook his head in a serious manner. 'I only have one guess left,' he said solemnly.

'Make it good,' I teased.

'It's … Alyce.' He nodded his head and smiled a smile of satisfaction.

My face went flush. How did he …? 'How?' I wondered aloud.

'Jesuits are blessed with the gift of names. It's one of the perks.'

I didn't know how to respond, so I changed the subject. 'The music is lovely,' I offered. 'I've always loved high mass.'

'Missa Cantata,' he clarified. 'High mass with music.'

I told him how my father would take me to high mass every Sunday, how we would all dress up in our Sunday's finest, how different things were when I was a little girl.

'Well Alyce, it's Sunday, they're celebrating high mass...'

'Missa Cantata,' I corrected.

'Missa Cantata,' he acknowledged. 'And you are wearing a very pretty dress. I bet it's your Easter dress,' he proffered. 'Those yellow flowers are very beautiful.'

'Thank you, Father,' I blushed. 'The bees like them, too. Sometimes there's so many buzzing around me, I think they're trying to pollinate me.'

Oh God, I couldn't believe I said that. I was so embarrassed, afraid that I said something inappropriate. But I was relieved when he started laughing.

'Then why don't we go inside, away from the bees, where we can listen to the music all proper?'

'I can't, Father,' I lamented. 'I'm divorced.'

'So what?' he asked. 'You're one of God's children. He loves you. He doesn't care about that. Now what do you say? Do you want to go inside?'

'Yes, Father,' I replied.

He took me by the arm, and led me up the stairs to the church's front door. As we ascended the stairs, I asked him why they were celebrating high mass.

'It's a glorious day when a lost child returns home,' he explained, as he opened the door for me. 'Welcome home, Alyce.'

4

Ex-Gay Ministries and Christianity
Caddyman's Story

This chapter presents the biography and beliefs of a Christian man, who narrates his inner conflict of being gay and Christian. In examining the emotional distress of the inherent paradox of being both Christian and gay, we observe how the two seemingly incompatible identities result in isolation and a desire to belong. This story is one which denotes the long, lonely craving to meet expectations, and such tensions are characteristic of stories found in early gay theology.[4]

Ex-gay Religious Conversion Therapy

The term 'ex-gay' relates to the task of an individual attempting to eliminate their homosexual desires by following a spiritual path aimed at promoting heterosexuality. The ex-gay movement was a pastoral element of conservative evangelical Christian intervention that practised conversion therapy with a view to changing the sexual identities of gay and lesbian Christians to heterosexual. *Exodus* was an umbrella organization of this movement, which grew until 230 local ministries served populations across the USA and Canada. Of these 230 ministries, Love In Action (LIA) was considered the biggest of its satellite ministries, and its ministry actually preceded Exodus International, being one of the pillars of its foundation. Formed in 1976, Exodus International ceased activities in June 2013, so for nearly four decades it promoted conversion practices aiming to rid Christians of the 'sin' of embracing a homosexual lifestyle.

'This Is What Love In Action Looks Like' (2011) is a real-life documentary, which follows the experience of a teenager, Zach Stark (16), whose parents enrolled him into the 'Refuge' programme aimed at teenagers. As Zach blogged about his fears about entering the programme against his will, the blog drew attention from LGBT-affirming activists who began to protest peacefully outside LIA headquarters. The documentary also reveals that LIA was violating state laws in relation to constitutional freedoms, and it ceased operating under that name in 2007. It was, however, the largest Christian organization in the world dealing directly with the 'issue' of homosexuality.

As a Christian organization, LIA initially offered a place of refuge and residence for those seeking behavioural therapy for issues such as drugs and alcohol misuse, but it became more popular for its work on pornography, sexual promiscuity and, especially, homosexuality. Those who graduated from the programme relating to homosexuality became known as 'ex-gay', while those who have spoken openly about their experiences during the programme, which include shame and trauma, call themselves 'ex-gay survivors'.

This chapter explores the experiences, beliefs and emotions of an ex-gay survivor, Caddyman. Not only is the narrator presented in this chapter a former adherent to the fundamentalist US-based Christian LIA programme, he was a *leader* and *director* of the programme which sought conversion to heterosexuality for homosexual Christians. Despite over 18 years preaching the possibility of conversion from the sin and shame of homosexual behaviour, his story ends in the present day where he has ultimately accepted his own homosexuality, affirmed his faith in Jesus and resides with his male partner. Today he acknowledges that 'the therapy did not work – I have never met a man who has changed from homosexuality to heterosexuality'.

Early Years

I was born in Colorado. I was the third child of my parents. Shortly after I was born they experienced marital problems and my dad decided to remove me and my siblings from the home. We went away to stay with our aunts, my sisters with one and I went to another. Our homes were good homes for us. We lived there about nine months.

In 1957 my parents got back together and we moved again for some kind of a fresh start. Life was okay for a season. But my mom went to work afternoons so we lived like our family was divorced and with my dad most of the time. I could tell there were deep problems but as a young boy in grade school I couldn't define them.

In 1965 my mom asked my dad to leave the home. We were devastated. There was no understanding of what had happened and no discussion about it. Mom came to pick us up from school one day, her boyfriend driving her car and we went away for a few days. When we returned dad had moved out.

We spent most of our free time cleaning the house, or going out to bars with mom and two of her boyfriends. We liked one of them; the other one, not so much. But dad was consistent in spending time with us on Sundays every week.

After one year, mom came to us and asked who we'd prefer she marry, Mike or Gary. We all said Gary. We had no more discussion, so one year after dad moved out, Mike moved in. Every facet of our lives changed. Household rules, daily routines, the entire atmosphere of our home went downhill. Mike was a dominant, harsh, drunk dictator. It seemed pretty clear he didn't like us, and he hated our dad.

Mom had two more children with Mike. Audrey was born in 1966, and Joanne was born in 1969 with Downs Syndrome. Of course, this changed our lives again. Mom stayed home from work now to take care of the babies.

My older sister moved out the day after her graduation from high school in June of 1967. She went to live with dad. My next sister got married when her boyfriend returned from Vietnam in 1969. When she moved out I was petrified! At that point, my dad asked me to move in with him. I was thrilled, and felt saved from the potential disaster of living longer in that home without my older sisters.

I spent the next couple of years with dad while I finished high school. I had a couple of different jobs and then after high school I got a job at the railroad. I had dated a couple of girls in high school – one in particular seemed to be the one I dated most often. We had several separations but seemed to always come back together.

In the above narration of his early childhood and teenage years, Caddyman does not make reference to religion and its role in his life. Before discussing the incompatibility of homosexuality and Christianity within his own life story, first I consider briefly the official positional statements from the main Christian churches.

The Problem of Homosexuality and Christianity

Positional Statements from the Christian Churches

The main official pronouncements on homosexuality from the Roman Catholic and Anglican denominations reveal Christianity as hostile towards homosexuality. Caddyman explains how his religious background as a child was Catholic, but he never felt like he belonged within the faith. Indeed, the notion of 'belonging' is one which is paramount to Caddyman's ex-gay conversion, which is later discussed. Regarding his Catholic background, Caddyman states:

All of my dad's family was Catholic. From his parents, siblings, and my cousins, all of them that I know of remained Catholic with the exception of my siblings and I. I discontinued going to church when I was about 18 then returned to more fundamentalist churches when I was 30. My mom became a Catholic in order to marry my dad but her heart wasn't in it and never was. She stopped attending church with us when I was about four years old. My dad took us all to church every Sunday. We all attended Catechism classes on Sundays. We went through First Communion and Confirmation.

Being raised Catholic gave me a foundation of believing in God and having a basic knowledge of Christianity from a Catholic view. Most of what I learned from him about faith and religion came from watching what he did rather than hearing what he may have thought or had to say. During my early years Catholic services were still in Latin. Then I remember them introducing guitar mass. I liked the newer more casual influence. I was never into the formality that was typical of Catholic Mass.

I had been raised in a Catholic home where my father was clearly sold out to God. But I could not seem to find a place for myself where I felt I really belonged. I gave up 'religion' when I turned 18 thinking I could now make it on my own.

Those who come to identify as non-heterosexual find themselves part of a heteronormative society which can cause inner conflicts and negative self-image. For those involved in religious communities, the difficulties are compounded as God can be assumed to be angry and unaccepting in relation to homosexual identities. Negative emotions and internal conflict figure prominently in the narratives of those who identify as gay and Christian, and this notion is presented in Caddyman's story and featured in early gay theology. Echoing Althaus-Reid and Yip's work detailed in Chapter 1, the question about compatibility between sexual and religious identities is at the core of our self-understanding as non-normative Christians, in which heterocentrism remains the marginalizing force. This conflict is highlighted explicitly within the context of ex-gay ministries, although in the ex-gay context, it is not a question of seeking compatibility between sexual and religious identities. The ex-gay ministry 'represents their sense of being in flux between identities' (Erzen, 2006, p. 3) and offers 'freedom' from this flux and the unwanted desires of homosexuality. Homosexuals are thus rendered as psychologically unwell people requiring healing from God.

The ex-gay movement reinforced the idea that homosexual tendencies and practices are an illness, long after legislative and psychological practices had retracted such statements. The history of homosexuality demonstrates how same-sex desire was considered a disease, an illness of the mind. Miller notes how during the 1950s and 1960s 'the era of "gay is sick" had arrived' (1995, p. 25). In his *Letter to an American Mother* (1935), Freud gave the following words of advice to a mother who was worried about her son being homosexual: 'Homosexuality is assuredly no advantage, but it is nothing to be ashamed of, no vice, no degradation. It cannot be classified as an illness.' In the same letter, he said, 'it is a great injustice to persecute homosexuality as a crime – and a cruelty too' (Freud, cited in Anderson, 2001, p. 23). Yet, despite Freud's assertion that homosexual people should not be criminalized and his doubt as to whether a 'cure' was available, several such 'cures' were developed with the intent of transforming 'sick' homosexuals to decent heterosexuals. These included extreme physical medical procedures such as castration, lobotomies, clitoridectomies and shock treatment as well as procedures to deal with the mental state of the 'sick' gay person, such as hypnosis. As we now live in more liberal times, the rights of homosexual-identifying individuals have been largely recognized in Western society and legislation, yet the majority of Christian denominations have not progressed nor revised their positional statements, which berate homosexual behaviours and identities as undesirable. Sadly, Goss's observation from 1993 still rings true today:

> For many lesbians and gay men, Christianity is perceived as the enemy. It is seen as socially oppressive, overtly antagonistic, and deliberately hostile. It legitimises cultural oppression and social violence. (1993, p. xiv)

To give examples of the oppression and hostility that Goss describes, we can view the positional statements from documents located in two mainstream Christian denominations: Roman Catholicism and the Anglican Communion.

Within official documents, the Roman Catholic Church de-nounces homosexuality as 'a troubling moral and social pheno-menon' (Congregation for the Doctrine of the Faith, 2003), and 'outside the confines of moral history or humankind ... we are face to face with a dissolution of the very image of man, whose consequences cannot but be extremely grave' (Ratzinger, 2004). In the pastoral letter *Homosexualitatis Problema* (1986), homosexuality is further described as a 'problem'. At the time of writing, the Roman Catholic Church, has not altered the 1986 declaration, 'although the particular inclination of the homosexual person is not a sin, it is a more or less strong tendency ordered toward an intrinsic moral evil; and thus the inclination itself must be seen as an objective disorder' (Congregation for the Doctrine of the Faith, 1986). Therefore, not only is homosexuality a 'problem', it is immoral: 'it is only in the marital relationship that the use of the sexual faculty can be morally good. A person engaging in homosexual behaviour therefore acts immorally' (Congregation for the Doctrine of the Faith, 1986). Equally problematic is the call to celibacy in Section 2359 of the Catechism of the Catholic Church (Roman Catholic Church, 1992): 'homosexual persons are called to chastity'. Indeed, the notion of a movement away from homosexuality towards heterosexuality often finds a compromising place, according to Erzen (2006), in which celibacy becomes a more attainable resolution. In his discussion of modern Catholicism, Mark Jordan notes how enforced celibacy denies 'gays any opportunity to experience their humanity' (2000, p. 38).

In the Anglican Communion, positional statements regarding homosexuality have been equally damaging, yet the Communion's wrangling with homosexuality has been a public affair. One statement from the House of Bishops describes homosexual practice as 'especially dishonourable' (Church of England, 1991, p. 18). The assembly of bishops at the Lambeth Conference in 1998 concluded that 'homosexuality is incompatible with Scripture'. Yet despite these positions, three events relating to homosexuality have led to a crisis within the Anglican Communion directly due to their grappling with the traditional theological understanding of homosexuality. First, the Anglican Church of Canada moved to bless same-sex unions in 2004; second, an openly gay priest in a longstanding homosexual partnership, Jeffrey John, had his appointment as Bishop of Reading withdrawn because of evangelical opposition; third, there was the ordination of a practising homosexual, Gene Robinson, as Bishop of New Hampshire by the US Episcopal Church. In 2004, the Communion published a document aimed at reconciling the international tensions between members of the Communion: *The Windsor Report*. In spite of the Windsor Report, these events have resulted in a deep and growing division within the worldwide Communion. The global West engages in a more tolerant dialogue on the question of homosexuality. By contrast, in the global South attitudes towards homosexuality remain negative in countries such as Nigeria with its large Christian population, where homosexuality remains illegal.

Such positional statements, which are vehemently anti-homosexual, have a negative impact on the gay-identifying Christian individual, as I discuss below. The positional documents do make a clear distinction between seeing the homosexual act as sinful, yet they are careful that 'the homosexual person' is not considered in such negative terms. *Homosexualitatis Problema* (Congregation for the Doctrine of the Faith, 1986), for instance, deplores the ways in which 'homosexual persons have been and are the object of violent malice in speech or in action' and advocates 'condemnation from the Church's pastors wherever it occurs'. There are strong statements concerning the dignity and worth of homosexuals, which call for respect for the 'intrinsic dignity of each person'. Although a positive move towards anti-discrimination against gay people, the document compounds the issue for gay-identifying Christians who feel torn between their sexuality and their faith.

Gay Theology: Exploring Being Gay and Christian

Michael Ford's *Disclosures* (2004) offers a series of moving, emotive and real-life stories that explore the duality of being gay and Christian. He notes that 'for some people, the words 'gay' and 'homosexual' still evoke the same reaction that the word 'cancer' once engendered – the unmentionable' (2004, p. 8). Within his compilation, the narratives of the varied contributors reveal the emotive language used to articulate the conflict of being gay and Christian. Ford names the emotions as he talks of shame, deception and psychological trappings. He provides examples of the 'psychological captivity' (2004, p. 10) experienced by gay Christians. Ford's text provides compelling and disturbing narratives and descriptions of torturous existence, vulnerability, enforced deception habits, ongoing personal vigilance and surveillance employed as part of their 'psychological survival kit for a homophobic world' (2004, p. 11).

In one example, a former Roman Catholic seminarian, Michael, describes how he has been 'physically, mentally and sexually abused in my life' and through his time in the seminary. He concludes, 'now I feel I have been spiritually abused as well' (2004, p. 17). Michael describes the psychological process he went through at the expense and encouragement of the seminary, in which he endured 'horrific psychological tests geared more to child rapists than seminarians' answering 'sickening questions that seemed entirely inappropriate' (2004, p. 19). The tests not only confirmed that Michael had a high sex drive and was indeed a gay man, they also concluded he was not a paedophile and not a danger to children, thereby erroneously and dangerously assimilating homosexuality with child abuse and paedophilia. Despite these rigorous and intrusive personal interventions, Michael still lost his place in the seminary. In another example, Sebastian, a Roman Catholic priest, describes his earlier periods of self-loathing and how he began to 'hate himself and to loathe the path he had chosen' (2004, p. 79). Sebastian recalls the 'many long months of loneliness and confusion' (2004, p. 79) and describes his homosexuality as follows:

> I think homosexuality was a wound I didn't want anybody to see. I wanted the cloth still to be covering it. My anxiety was that if anybody saw that wound, they would not have tried to heal or love it. They might have attempted to deepen the hurt. (2004, pp. 79–80)

It is significant to note how the notion of 'wound' arises. In Chapter 2, I discussed how practical theology serves as a response to a 'wound'. Michael's story reveals the failure of organized religion to understand the anxiety suffered due to being gay and Catholic. It confirms the need for practical theology to explore and respond to the hurt suffered by Christians due to the religion they practise.

To exemplify the importance of the churches' damaging statements and practices, Tigert discusses the shame of internalized homophobia among gay Christians, which can lead to negative self-image. She states:

Overcoming shame is part of the core spiritual and psychological work of overcoming homophobia ... it lies at the core of numerous psychological and spiritual concerns – depression, anxiety, addictions, isolation, violence, perfectionism, and spiritual alienation. (1999, p. 59)

Within the field of sociology, a study by Denise Levy and Patricia Reeves reveals further examples of identity conflict for those who identify as gay and Christian. One participant, Chad, quoted his pastor as saying, 'you could not be gay and go to church. You cannot be a Christian. You cannot inherit the Kingdom of God and be a homosexual. You will burn forever in hell' (2011, p. 59). Within the field of psychotherapy, Kelly Schuck and Becky Liddle analysed 66 surveys completed by respondents, aged between 18 and 65 and living in the United States. Among the respondents, 32 identified as gay men, 26 as lesbians, 7 as bisexual women and 1 as a bisexual man. When asked whether there was a conflict between their sexual identities and their religious lives, 64 per cent of the respondents noted such a conflict, which is described as follows:

Perhaps the most damaging consequence of anti-gay teachings was the belief, expressed by several respondents, that they would go to hell or that God had rejected them. Many felt judged by their religious communities ... The emotional consequences felt by LGB parishioners were often severe. Many reported feeling guilt and shame about their sexual orientation. Several reported severe depression, self-loathing, or suicidal ideation. Some felt unwelcome at their place of worship. Others felt excluded because of an exclusive valuing of, or focus on, heterosexual families. (2001, p. 70)

Gay Therapy

While attempting to overcome such shame, the practice of sexual conversion therapy has proven to compound issues of low self-esteem and self-image:

Employing techniques to strengthen willpower, encourage prayer, devalue homosexuality, and positively portray heterosexuality, such counsellors may, sadly, leave clients 'with such a degree of self-hatred' that not only will the clients' developmental journeys be terminated but so also may be their lives. (Cass, 1979, p. 229)

The limited references to overcoming shame concerning sexual identity in the psychotherapeutic texts become a significant characteristic of the literature in general. Yet it is this need for therapy that reflects how heteronormative Christian beliefs and practices impact on the lives of non-normative individuals. Time and again, therapists refer to the importance of dealing with shame, guilt and self-loathing.[5] Today, Caddyman himself is all too aware of the impact of heteronormativity in the lives of gay Christians:

I believe most of the gay people I've known do have a deep spirituality, or a strong negative reaction to religion – for some of the same reasons. The negativity comes from their pursuit of God and the rejection that has come from some of the religious people. The underlying statement in some of their minds is, if your God hates me I don't want anything to do with your God.

For those who were gay and willing to pursue a relationship with God by seeking conversion, the emotional and psychological damage the ex-gay movement had on them is incalculable. In one ex-gay survivor story, Jallen Rix (2010) narrates his ex-gay journey from what he describes as a damaging scheme, where his self-esteem was destroyed through the ex-gay ministry's view of homosexuality as negative combined with religious teaching which resulted in an unhealthy spirituality. Doug Haldeman states how sexuality conversion programmes 'often exacerbated already prominent feelings of guilt and personal failure among the counselees; many were driven to suicidal thoughts as a result of the failed reparative therapy' (1994, p. 224).

Precisely because we are dealing with the messy nature of human life experiences, the life story offered in this chapter will serve to highlight the cumulative impact of internalized homophobia and conflict between the sexual self and the religious self. In his own negotiation of sexual identity and religious beliefs, Caddyman reflects on how his life has been constrained by the conflict between his sexuality and his religion, yet his faith has also enabled some healing from his traumatic youthful experiences:

> I believe my life course has been constrained by the 'brand' of Christianity that I have lived in during these 30 years. I think if I had been in a more progressive faith it wouldn't have been such a problem for me. It's just that I entered into church life with people and leaders who have held on to a much more fundamentalist view of the Bible and Christian life.

> On the other hand, I must add that those years of fundamentalist Christianity have also given me some good things that are still with me such as a more balanced life and a deeper self-awareness. Also, being involved in a recovery type of ministry for so long helped me to more deeply process the damage and wounding from my childhood experiences with an unhealthy mom, and a broken home.

For those within the ex-gay movement, the belief is that heterosexuality is God's intent, and, in turn, heterosexuality enforces the binary of masculinity for men and femininity for women. Non-alignment with this binary can be shame-producing for those who do not or cannot live up to such expectations of performing masculinity or femininity. The ex-gay movement is antithetical to queer theory, which refutes such essentialist categories. Such radically distinct religious, political and sexual norms, including those of compulsory heterosexuality and internalized homosexuality, are played out in Caddyman's story. Tanya Erzen notes:

> Although men and women in ex-gay ministries do not and cannot envision homosexuality as a positive way to be, their lives also exemplify the instability of the religious and sexual conversion process. Their narratives of testimonial sexuality are performances that, while sincere, point to the instability and changeability of their own identities rather than serve as a

testament to heterosexuality. (2006, p. 14)

Editing Emotion

Ethnographers Tanya Erzen (2006) and Michelle Wolkomir (2006) analyse the religious and emotional socialization of the ex-gay movement in their research, which offers in-depth studies of the collective community of ex-gay evangelical groups. Erzen's research focuses on the everyday lives of men and women over the course of several years at *New Hope Ministries*, a residential ex-gay programme. Wolkomir's work signposts how a collective imposition of rules, sanctioning and modelling led the men to attempt to overcome their homosexuality through regulating their emotional expressions. In naming such emotional expressions, Wolkomir refers to feelings such as anger, fear and anxiety. Her study describes how supportive emotional expression allowed for 'mutual recognition, fostering collective identity and the feelings of belonging' (2006, p. 130). Yet, Wolkomir's description of emotions does not venture into the sexual exploration of fantasies or expressions of sexual desire.

Ford comments on how being aware of one's homosexual desires heightens one's negative self-image. He states, 'the growing awareness of such emotions often creates a sense of shame, low self-esteem and the fear of being considered abnormal' (2004, p. 12). For Caddyman, negative emotions featured prominently in his narrative. The inner conflict between being an 'authentic' Christian and his homosexual desires left Caddyman feeling confused, empty and alone. In his own words:

> I was quite aware of my salvation but did not really understand how to live my Christian life. I thought that a homosexual relationship with another Christian would work, but no matter how hard I tried, I still had a deep emptiness in my heart that no man could fill. The unhealthy way I was living ruined that relationship and I feared the most dreaded thing of all: being alone.

Rather than moving the individual men away from such negative emotions, it was the perpetuation of the negative aspect of these emotions within the ex-gay movement which meant that identity reconciliation was no longer an option. Some may argue, however, that the ex-gay ministry provided a safe place for gay Christians precisely because they were allowed to acknowledge their homosexual 'issues', rather than it being regulated through the compulsory silence which often permeates other Christian groups. Erzen acknowledges that despite the flux of being between identities, there is potential for such identity integration through the ex-gay programme, albeit temporary, as she notes, 'an ex-gay ministry becomes a place where these dual identities are rendered temporarily compatible' (2006, p. 3). Yet, it is important to remember that the goal of the ministry was the eradication, not the embrace of these homosexual 'issues', and 'ex-gay' narratives reveal how conversion therapy compounded feelings of self-hatred.

Wolkomir observes how the emotions of those involved in the ex-gay programme provide the foundations for three distinctive biographical paths, which can be used to describe the trajectory of ex-gay life-courses. These three pathways include belonging, bargaining and meeting expectations (2006, p. 56).

Belonging

Wolkomir's notion of 'belonging' is a significant element of ex-gay narratives and can be noted in Caddyman's story, as the majority of Caddyman's biography details how he sought refuge in finally being part of something that erases past hurts and isolation.

Caddyman's early years are described as beset with disruptive episodes, detailing his parents' marital problems and separation, and his mother's second marriage to a man he and his siblings did not like. His stepfather is described as 'a dominant, harsh, drunk dictator'. Using emotional expressions, he describes his unhappiness as a young boy:

> For five years life was a holy terror daily. It took everything in me just to survive the anxiety we lived in all the time. Mom and my stepfather fought all the time. The fights mostly broke out

after he got off work. He would come home and begin drinking, and mom would stir up some conflict and off they ran yelling, screaming, throwing things. This happened often each week. The other times, we all lived in terror that something would cause another fight so we tried as hard as we could to keep the peace.

Despite the emotive language expressing his youth as a time of turmoil and upset, Caddyman did not reveal any adolescent wrangling with his own sexuality. He simply states, 'I could tell there were deep problems but as a young boy in grade school I couldn't define them.' The inner conflict he details emerges during his adulthood, and Caddyman speaks openly about his emerging sexuality:

I began masturbating when I was about eight or nine years old. I had a friend who taught me about it and showed me how he did it. Much to my curiosity I never got involved with him in it and wasn't particularly drawn to do so when he did it. I thought of it as just a friend thing and due to my own naivety it just didn't enter my mind. It did, however, lay a foundation for me to practice it later on.

The dissatisfaction with his familial home situation changed as Caddyman moved in with his father. It is a search for a sense of belonging which later brought Caddyman to church. Wolkomir acknowledges this as a key feature of how gay men arrived at the ex-gay programme; taking on religious identity as a Christian becomes a 'resolution to rejectant isolation from childhood' (2006, p. 57).

Having given up on God at the age of 18, Caddyman describes his return to God at the age of 28: 'curiosity brought me to church,' and this curiosity is linked to his desire to belong. In describing his own Damascus moment, Caddyman comments:

I believed that God may have spoken to me! 'You don't have to live this way any longer,' a voice said to me on that night in 1982. Little did I know that such a simple statement during a church service would have a life-changing effect on me … The words I heard that night were not audible, but they were absolutely clear to me. God had just given me the hope that I needed in order to face the next season of my life. A new church that I had found offered something I had never seen before.

According to Wolkomir, belonging is based on the Christian promise of 'unconditional love and acceptance from Jesus, who wiped clean sins (what the men saw as wrong with themselves) and offered salvation' (2006, p. 57). Thus, a sense of belonging fills the void of rejection and isolation experienced through self-internalized homonegativity.

Ford's collection of stories demonstrates that isolation is a prominent feeling among closeted gay men. He comments:

> the homosexual understands his feelings but is tortured by the fear that anyone else should detect them. As a result he experiences social isolation, even when he is in the company of others ... He never feels relaxed enough to express his true feelings. (2004, p. 12)

Caddyman's own story is congruent with this: 'I just didn't believe I could be honest ... because of the tremendous Christian pressure to remain faithful, never be gay, and certainly not to admit a gay identity.'

A New Life in Jesus

In Caddyman's story, it is this account of turning to Jesus in which we see the first expressions of positive emotions in relation to of his own self-regard. He refers to the other Christians who supported him on his journey as his 'lifeline', and in this sense he felt he belonged. This sense of belonging served to counter his unhappy childhood experiences, where he felt 'in a continual anxious state'. Following his acceptance of Jesus and becoming part of a Christian community, he states, 'God knew I needed to feel like I belonged to this group' and 'God soaked me with relationships.'

Regarding his own beliefs, and despite the church's offer of freedom from sin and salvation, Caddyman felt a sense of belonging within an established community. This sense of belonging did not solve the inner turmoil he felt being gay and Christian. For Caddyman, the emptiness and fear of loneliness within the context of relationships continued to resurface:

> I had already come to believe that Jesus was my Savior and that the Bible was true, but my life was still completely consumed by a frantic search for some kind of completion in a significant relationship.

At the age of 19, Caddyman entered into a six-year marriage, which produced two daughters. He states:

> After dating for a couple of years in high school, marriage seemed to be the natural next step in my life. I was oblivious to the unresolved emotional baggage I was carrying into the marriage. I was very naive. I knew very little about my own sexuality, much less about how to deal with a hidden struggle with emotional attractions to other men. I was sexually a virgin before I married so my personal sexuality was something I had not physically explored. I had developed an addictive habit of masturbation and fantasies but that was the extent of my exposure to sexuality.

Following the end of his marriage, Caddyman began to explore and act upon his homosexual urges. He describes one sexual encounter with another man in almost sanitized, legal terms as he says, 'I committed homosexual adultery with him', depriving the idea of gay sex of any deep satisfaction either physically or emotionally. In a later discussion of his attendance at a Christian retreat, Caddyman describes sex as a negative behaviour: 'a Christian retreat offered an opportunity that I had looked for all my life: a social environment with others that was reflective of my Christian faith but did not involve sex, alcohol, or other negative behaviors'. Despite this, he entered into his first relationship with another male which lasted a couple of months, and then he continued to meet with other men in bars. He was dissatisfied with his promiscuous nature, as he states, 'after several sexual relationships and break ups I found that I had a deep seated fear – so great that I could not stand the thought of being without a "significant other" in my life.' Caddyman began a three-year relationship with another man which he describes as 'unhealthy'. Following this relationship, he sought to break his 'addiction to unhealthy relating' and confided in his pastor about his homosexuality. In an interesting phrase, Caddyman describes his intention: 'with a suspicious mind, I was testing him with my story'. I am unsure if his pastor did pass the test, but the pastor's response – 'I am not exactly sure what I can do but I will walk alongside you any way I can' – seems encouraging. Caddyman describes the sense of emotional satisfaction of being accepted by a heterosexual male:

> There was no judgment, no fear, just commitment. That was all I needed at the time. I wanted so much to be accepted in this strange and mysterious world of 'straight' men. His words felt like life-giving water to my parched, thirsty soul.

The church he attended during this period provided an environment in which Caddyman belonged and was accepted: 'Finally, I had found the place of belonging I wanted. God knew I needed to feel like I belonged to this group. God was giving me a purpose.'

Despite this sense of belonging, Caddyman comments 'all was not perfect', and the duel of having homosexuality in the mix with being Christian meant that he could not seek prayer at the altar. Within evangelical churches, the altar call is a practice in which individuals are invited to come forward to the altar to receive public prayer from others for their need. This prayer often includes the 'laying on of hands' and can be connected to a specific purpose such as seeking healing or to receive a blessing. In Caddyman's story, he avoided such prayer from others as he perceived his internal struggle as 'unchristian'. Even though he had never faced stigma from other Christian friends, Caddyman observes how 'I was fearful to seek prayer for my homosexual issues'. Moving away from seeking sex in bars with others, Caddyman 'did not look forward to a life of celibacy'. The fear of loneliness resulted in his bargaining for a better life and healthier relationship, and Caddyman attempted marriage for a second time:

> I wanted to find a special person with whom I could spend my

life. Since I accepted the perspective that I could not have a gay relationship, I figured I could try marriage to a woman again, this time from a different perspective.

Bargaining and Meeting Expectations

Wolkomir's second biographical journey is one of bargaining, in which the ex-gay men turn to Christianity in an attempt to 'bargain for a better life' (2006, p. 62). Through prayer, meditating on Scripture and seeking healing from homosexuality, the men attempt to ensure and safeguard a better future. Wolkomir gives an example of how this bargain with God works for an ex-gay man: 'If I believe in you and live by your Word, then you will help me to fix my life and make me happy' (2006, p. 62).

Caddyman notes the difficulty he had in praying or bargaining with God about his sexuality in his early days as a Christian. His desire for a better life would be for him to be rid of his homosexual desires, but also from his unpleasant childhood experiences: 'as a little child I felt so much hurt and pain because I perceived that I had been abandoned by my parents'. Through marriage and a variety of church experiences, Caddyman was rejecting his homosexuality and attempting to 'pass' as heterosexual, thus gaining the approval of God and his church. For Caddyman, bargaining with God for a better life would allow him to be free from his negative childhood experiences and self-unacceptance. Caddyman's emotive response exemplifies his inner turmoil and struggles with his own sexuality and faith:

> Oh my gosh, I sought prayer, prayed, begged, went to conferences, counseling and everything else I could discover. I was taught that through my Christian faith, God would honor my obedience and bring me to satisfaction someday, somehow. I also believed that if I ever entertained being gay again that it would severely damage my relationship with God. I never believed that I would lose my eternity with God, but that there would be an irreparable disconnect with God if I were actively gay.

The sin of homosexuality is so embedded within Christianity that it forms a barrier between an individual's relationship with his or her Creator. Indeed, although both Catholic and Anglican positional statements are clear that homosexual identification itself is deserving of compassionate pastoral care, engaging in homosexual acts is condemned. However, while a more accurate sentence would thus refer to the 'sin of homosexual acts', I maintain the notion of the 'sin of homosexuality' as this rings true in the general public consciousness. For Caddyman, the pain of bargaining, praying and begging was an act that attempted to secure a better future. It was a desperate endeavour to seek acceptance from God.

The final biographical pattern, 'meeting expectations' requires the ex-gay men to adhere to being members of a Christian community, as Wolkomir observes, 'church membership was mandatory for acceptance and respect in these communities' (2006, p. 66). Thus, the church offered an 'emotional promise' (2006, p. 89) which could provide effective help against the negative emotions which have been lived and experienced. Through the bargaining of his own sexuality and seeking the approval of other Christians, Caddyman got involved with ex-gay ministries. In 1986 he got involved with LIA as he took on a leadership position to work with their residential programme. He believed in his own conversion from homosexuality to such an extent that he remarried two years later, in 1988. With retrospective predictability, it was only a matter of time before the marriage ended:

> I finally publicly admitted to myself, to my wife, and to others that I am a gay man. My wife knew all of my story, so this was not new information. But I had spent our entire marriage trying to suppress my same sex desires. I did everything I knew how and subjected myself to many different venues, counselors, and deep personal reflection in an attempt to find success within my marriage. All, to no avail. I decided to separate from my marriage and file for a divorce. It was very painful for both of us to do this. I felt I had no option any longer. There was no way I could ever go back to the life of an ex-gay man. Now that I was living authentically, I had to continue applying this to my personal life fully.

Interestingly, Caddyman did not dwell in detail about his time as an LIA director, nor did he offer any regret for his part in this organization.

Today, Caddyman feels he is in a place where he can accept his homosexuality and realize the 'toxic effects' his former Christian beliefs had on his own self-worth. After many years of attempting to deny his homosexual identity, he realizes it is a part of him he cannot escape from, and he feels grateful to God for this realization:

I feel of great value to the Lord and to His work. I have a sense of belonging, personhood and relationship with others. Homosexuality is a part of my emotional, physical, and spiritual history and present. It will not be erased as though it never existed! I found that most of the anxiety I experienced within my marriage was connected to being a gay man married to a straight woman. I thought those issues would be resolved, but finally realized they were due to the inherent nature of being gay.

Undoing Emotions

Significant for this chapter is the work of Alison Jagger (1989), who stresses the importance of emotion in all research, making redundant the perceived invisible dividing line between reason and emotion. Although closely aligned with its synonym 'feelings', 'emotions' in research can easily be dismissed as a subjective indulgence, guided by temporal spirits and moods. The psychological 'emotion' is often blurred with the physiological 'feeling'. Yet, my experience is that emotion is paramount as it fuels the researcher and allows the researcher to conduct ethical research based on values. Jagger gives examples of some emotions which fuel a researcher's investigations: shock, sadness, pain, trauma, compassion, outrage (1989, p. 161). She details what she calls 'outlaw emotions', those that are conventionally subversive of traditional research methods or unaccepted in relation to dominant ideologies (1989, p. 160). It is these 'outlaw emotions', Jagger argues, that are central to feminist (and, I would add, queer) enterprise:

> Outlaw emotions stand in a dialectical relation to critical social theory ... Feminists need to be aware of how we can draw on our outlaw emotions in constructing feminist theory and also of how the increasing sophistication of feminist theory can contribute to the re-education, refinement, and eventual reconstruction of our emotional constitution. (1989, p. 160)

Jagger's argument highlights how emotions are socially constructed on many different levels: through interpretations, observations, judgements, evaluations and settings. Martha Nussbaum (1989) concurs with Jagger in asserting that emotions are social constructs. Moving beyond the traditional perception that emotions are an inner, natural part of our personal make-up, both Nussbaum and Jagger, writing in the same year, consider emotions to be contrivances in the form of social constructs:

> The apparently individual and involuntary character of our emotional experience is often taken as evidence that emotions are presocial, instinctive responses, determined by our biological constitution. This inference, however, is quite mistaken ... Emotions are most obviously socially constructed in that children are taught deliberately what their culture defines as appropriate responses to certain situations. (Jagger, 1989, p. 15)

> We learn how to feel and we learn our emotional repertoire. We learn emotions in the same way that we learn our beliefs – from our society. But emotions, unlike many of our beliefs, are not taught to us directly through propositional claims about the world, either abstract or concrete. They are taught, above all, through stories. Stories express their structure and teach us their dynamics. These stories are constructed by others, and then taught and learnt. But once internalized, they shape the way life feels and looks. (Nussbaum, 1989, p. 217)

This idea of emotions as social constructs is one which does not deny or elide the true side-effects of feeling an emotion. An emotional response to a traumatic event, for instance, is not premeditated and carefully considered before it is expressed. What is meant by the social construction of emotions is that it is not the emotional response – 'the feeling' – that is socially constructed, but rather it is the emotion as a collective expression of the feeling that is a construct. In light of this realization that emotions are socially constructed, Nussbaum solidifies the idea of temporality in terms of narrating one's own story and reviewing one's emotions: 'if stories are learned they can be unlearned. If emotions are constructs, they can be dismantled' (1989, p. 218).

Retelling life stories is a common feature of the ex-gay programme, as the stories of being healed from homosexuality involve multiple retellings over time in the form of testimonies. The ex-gay ministry mindset of healing, deliverance and freedom provided the themes that dominated Caddyman's previous life-story narratives.

There is a clear queer connection between Butler's theory that repetitions of gender performativity require rupture, disruption, dismantling and Nussbaum who states that emotions can be deconstructed. Moreover, it is this dismantling of previous biographies and beliefs that is central to ex-gay survivor stories. Ex-gay survivors need to undo previously understood beliefs and self-images. Ford offers words of caution when dealing with emotions and feelings that touch the core of our inner lives, and he warns 'if these powerful emotions are sealed off or disguised, they can cause psychological and spiritual damage' (2004, p. 13). Undoing emotions as part of religious testimony allows the expression of powerful feelings that are central to us as living beings. Undoing emotions also serves to provide resolution to previous damage done by concealing such deep feelings.

Queer investigations, as indebted to feminist research paradigms, give weighting to the importance of emotions in theology. I suggest that emotions can be useful in the reconsideration of the production of male theology, as I explore in the next section.

Revisiting Male Theology: Having the Balls and the Fear of Impotency

Mats Alvesson and Kaj Sköldberg (2009) refer to gender-related ideas about 'masculine' research being more quantitative and 'feminine' research favouring a qualitative approach, contrasting masculinized scientific 'reasoning' with perceived feminized methods of emotion and feeling. Their apparent gender bias notes how feminist methods are

> characterized by a qualitative approach, in which the subjectivity of both the researcher and the subjects studied is central – in the first case through empathy and commitment, and in the second through personal experience. (2009, p. 242)

Ann Oakley complained about male research methodology that ignored emotive content, critiquing such absence in what she calls a 'sociology of feeling and emotions' (1981, p. 40). Similarly, Karl Nunkoosing shares the same concern and advocates a focus on not just the content of the story, but how the stories are told (2005, p. 705).

Silvia Gherardi and Barry Turner denote the irony of such gender-related research camps in their text 'Real Men Don't Collect Soft Data' (1987), which challenges the traditionally perceived research gender binary. In a similar vein, James Nelson argues:

> In the world of male achievement, hard facts mean more than soft data. Men listen more readily to data from the 'hard sciences' than to the soft, seemingly mushy information and theories from the 'people sciences'. (1988, p. 37)

The narratives from ex-gay participants could be best located within the field of men's studies in religion, as the life stories explore the sexual construction and deconstruction of masculinity, with its heterosexual privilege.[6] Nelson posits that masculine spirituality is categorized by separation from a God who is 'distant, cold, controlling, unavailable' (1988, p. 45). He also argues that men are rendered female by belonging to a church that is feminine and is referred to as 'she'. The female church thereby renders impotent the ideas of men inheriting power, control and dominance from a male God. Nelson substantiates this point by affirming that 'a male God penetrates us. But to be penetrated by anyone or anything, even

God, amounts to be womanized' (1988, p. 45). In his own personal reflection, Nelson notes how he himself saw God as 'beyond' rather than 'within'. He describes how he was reared on a male-orientated theology which puts 'emphasis on mystery that is external and radically transcendent of the self' (1988, p. 35). This external potency becomes a defining feature of male theology, especially noted within ex-gay ministries. Nelson's own spiritual journey saw himself as a penetrator:

> For most of my life I assumed automatically that the proper object of my spiritual life was really 'out there,' rather than a mystery dwelling deeply within me. It was something I had to penetrate. My desire was to grasp, to understand, to analyse. (1988, p. 35)

A call for a male theology that recognizes an eradication of binary male/female, heterosexual/homosexual, outside/inside is one which Nelson began to consider in 1988 but without the helpful tools of feminist and queer theory. Yet, even alongside such developments and the arrival of more liberal politics, LIA continued to operate under that heading until 2012. The ex-gay ministry reinforced traditional masculine theologies through the promotion of patriarchal ideologies and the expectation that heterosexual hegemony was sanctioned by God. Consequently, the dissolution of the organization served to blot the pages of masculine theology, allowing space for a reconsideration of masculinity and spirituality. Reflecting on Nelson's idea of men privileging *hardness*, rather than *softness*, it is apparent that ex-gay ministries, in their promotion of masculinity and regulation of femininity, embrace this 'hardness'. Nelson also discusses how men embrace linearity and history rather than cycles and nature:

> Men also honor straightness and linearity. To be sexually straight for a male in a homophobic society is crucial to being a real man. History has always been more important to male-dominated societies than has nature, and history seems to be linear ... Nature on the other hand appears to be cyclical. (1988, p. 37)

With a queer lens we can observe the significance for this desire for 'hardness' as typical, as it is the form of masculinity which the ex-gay movement embraces. For ex-gay ministries, being masculine equals rigidity and straightness. The same principles underlie the imagination of male genitalia. Regarding male (hetero)sexuality, it is the firm erection which is necessary for sexual success in terms of procreation. For heteronormative society, it is straightness which is necessary for social and religious success. Nelson advocates a move away from the genitalization of male sexuality:

> When we who are male think of sexuality, we usually think of 'sex,' and that means genital experience. We do not think first, or primarily, of sensuousness or of an emotionally intimate relationship. (1988, p. 34)

As Isherwood thanked Althaus-Reid for moving feminists away from the womb and focusing on the vulva (2003, p. 101), I thank Nelson for encouraging men to get over the erection and focus on emotional relationality.

Of course, we must remain carefully critical not to consider men as a homogeneous group with shared experiences, yet this hegemonic traditional heterosexual masculinity was the ideal upheld in the ex-gay conversation programme. Accounts exist which detail the ex-gay focus on the promotion of traditional masculinity, such as sports, constructing or camping (see Mendiger, 1983; 2000), yet this demonstrates how the movement sees gender as socially constructed rather than biological. These activities focus on performance, endurance, strength and survival. Erzen notes how these masculine experiences can be linked to religious transformation:

> The practices of basketball or camping become sacred rituals in the service of developing a new identity. The idea is that if they first recuperate their gender identity through masculine ritual practices like basketball, heterosexuality, masculinity's natural correlation, will soon follow. For many, climbing a mountain or scoring a basket is a transforming religious experience. (2006, p. 109)

Ex-gay men who successfully participate in such traditionally heterosexual masculinized areas believe a conversion to hetero-sexuality will reconcile their sexual and spiritual identities. The myth is perpetuated within ex-gay rhetoric that proving one's masculinity affirms one's sexuality, and the promise of normalized heterosexuality becomes within reach. Within this assumption of hegemonic masculinities as the ideal to embrace, there is an expectation in the paradigm that gay men equal effeminate men. In reality, this is not the case, as the existence of 'straight-acting' men, macho leather men, bears and other non-effeminate gay men ruptures the expectations of such monolithic categories.

Updating the academic literature on masculine spiritualities since Nelson, more recent discussions come from Joseph Gelfer (2009). Gelfer's work explores masculine spirituality in a similar context to how feminists and queer theologians have approached theology with personal experiences and the question of identity at the forefront of debate. Gelfer offers an overview of historical masculine spirituality and moves to discuss contemporary masculine spiritualities from evangelical, Catholic and gay perspectives. One of the features of masculine theology which he highlights is how the fear of figurative impotency is one of the major anxieties within concerns about Christian masculinities and male theology (2009, p. 49). An appeal to masculine spirituality embraces traditional masculine stereotypes, which the ex-gay movement promotes and which Nelson sought to erase. In one contemporary example, Gelfer mobilizes the example of 'Muscular Spirituality' within evangelical church groups which use a sporting analogy to denote gender separation and to appeal to the male audience in order to further the development of masculine-patriarchal spirituality. In brief, masculine spirituality rejects flaccidity as insignificant and continues to worship the erection. Masculine spirituality perpetuates patriarchy by eliding the significance of emotions.

To return to the story of our protagonist here, the certification and seal of heterosexual approval comes in the form of marriage, yet it is during Caddyman's second marriage that his emotions began to conflict once again. Wolkomir notes that for ex-gay adherents 'being Christian meant being heterosexual, getting married and having children' (2001, p. 408). The inner conflict of being gay and married to conform to Christian ideals resulted in anger, which was inappropriately expressed towards his wife:

The hurts, rejections, and difficulties of my past relationships with women and men came to a head within my new marriage. Soon I realized that I was feeling a deep seated anger toward my wife that I did not understand. My critical heart toward her was unfounded in anything she had done. She was kind, considerate, loving. She really was not doing anything that would merit my responses.

When the marriage ended, Caddyman began to feel more positive:

I was asked if I was willing to pray about the marriage. I said I had prayed my guts out for the last 2 years. I believed it was insane to continue believing something would change. After we separated, I engaged in a relationship with a man I had previously met. The freedom, the intimacy, and the connection I now felt with him was something I never believed I'd ever experience in my life. After we connected I finally saw the amount of negative energy that was expended every day just to keep myself afloat within the marriage. I no longer have that within my daily life. I feel relieved, lighter, and finally have a sense of healthiness within my life.

Caddyman testifies how reconciling the conflict between his sexual and spiritual identities has resulted in a healthier self-image. With the focus on men and homosexuality which permeates the ex-gay ministry's ideology, the analogy of testimony is vital to identity construction within ex-gay contexts.

In Christianity, testimony has been a major characteristic within the evangelical movement. Constructing and reconstructing testimonies is a feature of the individual Christian narrative. Erzen notes how the format of the testimony model is familiar to ex-gay stories and they are encouraged to use this to express their journey from sinner to saved:

Ex-gays are encouraged to confess and testify as part of the process of sexual transformation ... The testimony, with a sin and redemption narrative, has long been a hallmark of evangelical Christianity. Testifying for men and women ... was central to their process of sexual and religious conversion, illustrating their stories before and after dedicating their lives to Jesus, from sinner to saved. The testimony is the narrative form into which all ex-gays eventually fit their lives before and after becoming Christians. (2006, pp. 11–12)

Erzen reminds us of the importance of testimony within the ex-gay movement and how biographical narratives can often be inflexible: 'a person's testimonial narrative of conversion becomes more structured and even rigid the longer he or she has been involved in an ex-gay ministry' (2006, p. 12).

The story of Caddyman and the wider consideration of the ex-gay movement are stories which are thankfully becoming rarer, as, certainly within Western society, sexuality can now be discussed alongside religion, yet the positions of the churches have not progressed so far. Queer activists have paved the journey to where we currently are, but the legacy of all those Christians who have learnt to hate themselves through their religion is one which is still rife in countries and communities around the world. Ex-gay stories map the journey of gay men from the fear of God's judgement to the longing for salvation. Caddyman's story is one which echoes the story of original sin. His ex-gay narrative presented in this chapter substantiates the constructed nature of the narrative form, and, significantly, the temporality of a belief narrative or theology. Not only are emotions embedded within narratives, stories also generate in their readers emotions which are not always documented in written form. Aware that our stories are enmeshed with other stories, listening to others and integrating our own story is an ongoing task. This task acknowledges the exercise of constant editing and rewriting of our life stories and beliefs, and prioritizing the expression of emotions as signifiers of ourselves as humans and thinkers.

Ex-gay stories often have multiple retellings in the form of testimonies. Erzen's position does not take account of the multiple retelling of stories and how narratives evolve and change. It is worth viewing testimonial accounts as emerging from fluid, highly subjective and changing interpretations of events. Denise Levy and Patricia Reeves state the need for a postmodern understanding of identity, so that we can bring 'a fresh perspective to the existing literature by viewing the construct of identity as fluid, ever-changing, and complex rather than as fixed, unitary, and stable' (2011, p. 55).

Erzen observes in her own study how the social construction of testimony becomes part of a collective identity. In the ex-gay setting, the grand narrative is one of being able to overcome homosexuality and lead a true Christian life which no longer displeases God and the church. Erzen discusses how each individual narrative feeds into this ex-gay grand narrative, as listening to other stories provides a regulatory structure and framework for each participant to construct his own story. The temporality of one's own individual biography and self-narrative is situated with the backdrop of social and collective frameworks of the ex-gay movement, as Erzen details:

> As they hear other testimonies through day-to-day interactions in the program, they learn to strategically position and locate their own lives into a similar framework of sinner and saved. (2006, p. 12)

> There is also a social and collective aspect to testimony, and giving one becomes a rite of initiation into the religious world of a ministry. These stories of trauma and healing are central to the culture of therapy that predominates … ex-gay ministries. (2006, p. 13)

'Testimony' itself is sexually and anatomically apt, especially when one considers the etymology of the word 'testament'. Isherwood defines this adequately:

> The term 'testament' is derived from testicles. In order to swear an oath, to tell the truth, one had to hold one's testicles and swear. Women were therefore debarred from any public or private activity that demanded the taking of oaths since they did not have the balls to tell the truth! (2003, p.144)

With a continued focus on the genitalization of men's spirituality, Roland Boer's text 'Too Many Dicks at the Writing Desk, or How to Organize a Prophetic Sausage-Fest' reminds us that man's ability to write is linked to his potency: 'masculinity and power are determined by one's phallic ability to write' (Boer, 2010, p. 98) and that 'writing, understood as a complex socio-economic phenomenon, means power' (2010, p. 99). The ability to create one's own history, one's own masculinity and construct one's own narrative is power:

> So we have a situation where the scribe's cock is his very firm, ironlike pen, the implement that rests on his balls and constructs the world of the text. That pen(is) is the implement of power, a power that is inescapably masculine due to the very identity of the pen(is) itself. Rigid, solid, unchallengeable, is it not? (2010, p. 100)

Balls are synonymous with bravery and strength – just note the colloquial phrase, 'having the balls to do something' – while the penis shaft and its potential potency denotes power. It is not insignificant to note that these virtues of strength, bravery and power are ones articulated through the ex-gay ministry's ideology as noted above in the discussion of ritual masculinity as a step towards heterosexuality. Like Nelson, Martin Stringer has pointed out that focusing exclusively on the genitals results in the alienation of emotions: 'sexuality ... is not focused simply on the genitals but is a function of the whole body, it permeates the whole of life and brings the erotic into every aspect of every relationship' (1997, p. 32).

A true sexual theology will be one which acknowledges that the experience of doing sexual theology will be more pleasurable and satisfying with a powerful emotional engagement too. We need to share our stories of pain, trauma, exclusion, isolation and survival. Ultimately, sharing one's intimate experiences of life and one's relationship with God does take balls, not of the testicular kind, but concerning the courage it takes to tell our stories. We tell our stories of survival not to be alone, and a theology based on sexual storytelling is a sacred act which lets others in. For ex-gay men, surviving the conflict of sexual and spiritual identities, as well as 'religious abuse' (Rix, 2010) is an example of human bravery. Caddyman himself notes:

> I think that people who are gay have learned to live in such challenging circumstances of growing up gay in a straight man's world that there is a searching and depth that come as a result of those circumstances.

The theologian, Phillip Kennedy, reminds us that Christianity 'is overwhelmingly the product of men's pens' (2006, p. 200). When engaging with life stories, the sexual theologian acknowledges that pens run out of ink and penises are not always rigid. Embracing emotions in the production of theology is neither linear nor circular, it is a theology which is happy to colour out of the lines and circles. Promoting a belief system on such rigid objects will result in theological impotency. In the example of Caddyman in this chapter, having and holding the pen to keep rewriting his story is temporal, as temporal as the ink in a pen or a male erection.

Theological power is not about the pen; it is about engaging in a more holistic person-centred approach to producing theology. Telling one's own story is central to one's self-understanding and the formation of one's beliefs. Emotive language employed to describe experiences of pain, trauma and sexual struggles demands that religion is more flexible and less rigid and erect. A theology based on sexual stories provides a space for Christianity to become more flexible, and this flexibility provides room for our subjective humanity. A theology such as this is built on the instability of radical vulnerability, and that is truly a queer thing.

5

BDSM and Christianity
Cath's Story

BDSM is a portmanteau term to denote the practice of bondage, discipline, dominance, submission, sadism, masochism. This chapter explores fetishism, faith, bondage and beliefs in the life of a practising Christian, heterosexual-identifying female who engages in BDSM practices. Our UK-based protagonist here chose the pseudonym Cath Artic, as catharsis is central to her understanding of the BDSM practices she engages in. Cath's story is therefore a confessional act as she presents her non-normative practice as a source for theology:

> A fetish theology may be in itself a kind of confessional act, for confession is the act of confronting truths of unequal legitimisation orders; the act of presenting theologically marginalised subcultures and their condemned truths to the authorised truth of dogma. The theologian of sexual salvation grounding her discourse in fetishism, assumes then the role of becoming a confessing subject and a confessor herself, professing her vocation of reflecting from the margins of sexual orthodoxy. (Althaus-Reid, 2003a, p. 41)

Early Years and Adolescence: Dualism and Decency

Cath's story begins with vivid memories of her childhood, which were always associated with church. She describes how 'church became a major feature in my life'. The church she describes was very conservative and traditional, and her mother and father were active in the church as elders: 'women wore hats, they were very evangelical, very "Bible-based", lots of old gospel songs, an organ, and certainly no drums!' Such a conservative exposure to religion had to be carefully upheld, and Cath describes how her parents encouraged her to become a 'good' girl, resulting in a regulation of any 'bad' influences:

> My parents (particularly my mum) were very keen that I should only have 'good', Christian influences. We had no TV. I had a couple of friends, but I spent a lot of time by myself, or with only my parents. If they were attending some kind of Christian convention, I went along. Mostly, I was the only child in the room, and so I spent a lot of time with adults listening to and being involved in their theological conversations.

Yet despite Cath's parents' attempts to ensure she was a 'good' girl and that her influences were carefully monitored, this did not protect her from childhood sexual exploitation by her older teenage cousin. She notes:

> One of my older teenage cousins would occasionally touch me inappropriately during these years. When he visited, he would sequester me away to play 'mummies and daddies'. He'd make me lay on top of him, and put his hand down my knickers and stroke my bum. I remember feeling bad about doing something 'naughty', that I was pretty sure I'd be told off for doing, and so I didn't want to do it. I said 'No', but he'd just cajole me until I complied with him. I remember telling my mum about it, and hoping she'd do something, but she just told me to tell him 'no'.

Cath recalls how these events occurred on approximately three occasions. The episodes left her feeling bad and that she was 'the guilty party'. She reports that she did not find the experiences arousing, and that she began to dread his visits. These 'abusive episodes', as Cath describes them, stopped once her older cousin found his first girlfriend.

Robin Bauer's text *Queer BDSM Intimacies: Critical Consent and Pushing Boundaries* (2014) is based on his own fieldwork (interviews and observations) with lesbian, gay, bisexual and transgender participants. In contrast to my work here, Bauer's work does not explore the practices of heterosexuals, nor is it based on his participants' religious identities. Nevertheless, Bauer observes how 'certain feminist and psychological theories that seek to pathologize BDSM behaviour have linked it to the experiences of sexual abuse' (2014, p. 102). Similarly, Nordling et al. (2000) have explored the prevalence and effects of self-reported childhood sexual abuse among males and females who engage in sadomasochist practices. Their work reports that there is a higher frequency of reported abuse among those who engage in SM practices, compared to those of the general Finnish population where the study was undertaken.

As a young Christian, Cath discusses how her belief system was very much based on regurgitating the words and proclamations of her parents, which were 'quite fundamentalist and conservative'. She notes how certain behaviours and lifestyles were considered 'bad':

> Homosexuality was bad. Sex outside of marriage was bad. Abortion was a sin. I learned that if I questioned anything, I would be roundly told off for not being a 'good Christian', and that I'd better say what I was expected to if I didn't want to be told off.

Judith Daniluk and Nicolle Browne (2008) explore the impact of traditional religious doctrine on women's sexuality through research-based work with US/Canadian women. Their work exposes how 'religious teachings provide the framework within which people judge the rightfulness or wrongfulness of their sexual feelings, fantasies, and activities, as well as those of others' (2008, p. 131). As we observe how Cath felt guilty for the sexually abusive episodes she experienced at the hands of her cousin, we note how this emotion of guilt relating to any sexual activity is often due to religious belief, and this coheres with the broader evidence for religiously induced guilt as a result of sexual activity. Daniluk and Browne state: '[Christian women] feel guilty for their sexual thoughts, fantasies, feelings and behaviors that do not fit within the rigid and oppressive constraints advocated within these moral traditions' (2008, p. 136). A traditionally conservative Christian theology for young adolescent female development is one which is decent and promotes 'good' girl discourses:

> Being based upon or interpreted through patriarchal lenses, the common elements related to women's sexuality in the religious teachings ... include: a dualistic separation between mind and body, spirit and sexuality; an emphasis on intercourse and procreation in circumscribing the definition and purpose of sex; valuing and treasuring of virginity; insistence on sexual exclusivity between married partners; sanctions against sex outside of marriage; and admonishment of masturbation, sexual fantasies and homosexuality. (Daniluk and Browne, 2008, p. 134)

Sonya Sharma (2011) discusses in more detail 'good' girl sexuality within the church. Although she does not engage with a discussion of BDSM practices at all, Sharma's work does explore the relationship between women's sexual lives and their identities as Christian. She explores the double bind for women in terms of being faithful to their Christian values and seeking out sexual pleasure. Sharma observes how the idea of 'good' girl discourse represents a conventional Christian view on sexuality, which is upheld in Christian communities and can be challenging for Christian women.

Against a largely similar backdrop of such an uncompromising religious upbringing, as described by Daniluk and Browne above, Cath does recall one curious element of her teenage years, which leaves her amused. She notes how her mother 'loved sexy lingerie and nightwear'. She comments, 'she would always ensure that I had beautiful underwear. It was a slightly odd thing for a teenager who wasn't supposed to show that sexy lingerie to anyone!'

Masturbation and Indecency

Cath describes how it was through her own exploration of faith and sexuality that she began to notice the emergence of a 'split life'. Her private sexual practices and her public decent Christian persona for her parents led to duality. She notes how she maintained the 'good' girl persona for her parents, yet in private, she began to discover her own sexuality:

> I was a very 'good' child and teenager. I didn't rebel at all – I just went to church, went to school, did my homework, and did what I was told! Oh, and I did a *great deal* of masturbating! I had a very active imaginative sex life. All my fantasies revolved around dominant men. Often there was force involved in my fantasies. I used to feel constantly guilty about the masturbation and did a lot of repenting of my 'sin', and promising God that I wouldn't do it anymore. Those resolutions never lasted very long!

Amy Mahoney and Olivia Espín explore how representations of female decency for Christian women are based on unrealistic representations of Mary, as submissive, obedient and ready to self-sacrifice. They argue that 'dualistic, negative thinking that has compartmentalized women's sexuality and spirituality in terms of Madonna or whore needs to be challenged' (2008, p. 3). Elsewhere, Mahoney extends this by arguing that for adolescent Christian women, sexuality and spirituality are irreconcilable:

> Many Christian women have grown up with the message that they can be spiritual, but not sexual or they can be sexual, but not spiritual. They cannot be both simultaneously. They can be like the Madonna (and this is preferred) or if they express sexual pleasure and freedom, they will be considered 'loose' women. (2008, p. 91)

Guilt and Regulation

The Hite Report published in the 1970s highlighted the taboo around female masturbation 'most women said they enjoyed masturbation physically (after all, it did lead to orgasm), but not usually psychologically' (Hite, 1976, p. 53). With reference to masturbation from a Christian perspective, Julia Collings notes how, for women, 'no sin is greater than the desire to masturbate (masturbation *itself* being completely out of the question)' (1998b, p. 64) and Patricia

Jung offers a Roman Catholic perspective on female sexuality, observing that 'masturbation is judged particularly wrong for women' (2000, p. 37). As completely contrary to the pure, decent ideal of womanhood, masturbation is likely to produce feelings of guilt and shame. Furthermore, Jung accounts for this construction of sexual goodness among women in Roman Catholicism as the reason why many women do not enjoy sex: 'the absence of sexual joy in so many women's lives is in part a consequence of the way "good sex" has been constructed in Christian moral traditions' (2000, p. 33). The resulting feelings of shame are often the outcome of sexual activities in 'decent' Christian discourses on female sexuality. In her work on women's experiences of sexuality within church communities, Sharma notices how shame and guilt actually serve as regulatory forces on Christian women's bodies within church communities:

> Shame and guilt are socially produced and are experienced powerfully at the site of women's bodies. A well-managed body within many churches is in control of sexual desires and experiences, and presents itself as feminine through, for example, appropriate dress. Shame and guilt combine to function as an internal compass for how many Christian women present their selves and live out sexual experiences. (2011, p. 67)

Cath describes how her early adult years involved experimenting with sex with various men, one of whom later became her husband. She describes how, once engaged to be married, she tried to cease sexual activity with her future husband, as she felt that she should attempt to retain a standard of 'decency' before marriage:

> Women in particular are taught that having sex before marriage is dirty. It's the ultimate sin – not only are you sinning against your future husband, by ripping away your virginity from him, but you are committing the ultimate sin against God, because your body is supposed to be the temple of the Holy Spirit. Interestingly this teaching is levelled overwhelmingly at women. Even in the church, men aren't charged with remaining 'pure' with anything near the pressure that is placed upon women.

The idea of shame for 'good' Christian women can be further situated in wider discussions on shame within religion. Stephen Pattison (2000) explains how Christianity has produced and exploited shame. His hypothesis is that Christianity uses shame to enhance order and control: 'shame can be used as a very effective means of manipulating people into obedience and compliance in the interests of the powerful who identify those interests with the will of God' (2000, p. 229).

The language used to describe the relationship of shame to Christians is at odds with the consensuality and mutuality of BDSM, as although 'obedience' and 'compliance' are mutual signifiers to both BDSM and Christianity here, the idea of manipulation is not. Power is carefully negotiated and regulated within BDSM, but not within religious communities.

For Cath, the pressure to attempt to maintain holy goodness was futile, and it is only when she abandoned such attempts that she discovered God's grace:

Looking back, most of my 'faith' was spent trying to assuage my guilt, and trying to be 'good'. I was never quite good enough, though. I decided that it was time to live my life. If I was going to have a faith, it would be something that I would explore on my own terms, and it would be truly mine, not something that my parents had forced on me. I discovered different interpretations of the Bible than those I'd been taught as a child, and realised that they made so much more sense to my conscience than the hard, fundamental ways I'd been taught.

I discovered Grace for the first time. I realised that by trying to live by 'rules', I'd fallen into a very old trap of trying to be 'good enough' for God – something I was never going to be. The God I'd known wasn't actually someone I'd liked – and for good reason. He was just waiting to catch me out being bad so he could punish me, and to be honest that God wasn't someone I wanted to know. But the God I discovered wasn't like that at all. He was someone who loved me, who wanted me, who was voracious for me. I felt completely seduced by him.

'Polykinkery', BDSM and Christianity

BDSM has been theologized by linking the practice to Christ's cross on Calvary (Laccetti, 2015), and the parallels between a dominant God and a submissive Christ (or Christian) are not complex ones to draw. Cath herself conceptualizes the relationship between God and Christians in the same dual relationship of dominant/submissive:

> As a submissive, I think it's quite easy to relate that to being submissive to God, and see Christ's submission to his Father. I sometimes wonder whether it's more difficult for a Dominant person to reconcile their orientation with their faith – particularly if they are a Dominant woman, something that traditionally would be frowned upon in many Christian circles. Submission is something that's often mentioned in the Bible – wives to their husbands, Christians to God, Christ to the Father. It's not difficult to draw the parallel.

For Cath, God's creation of our bodies is a source for celebration. She regards current Christian teachings and the perpetuation of 'good' Christian (female) sexuality as quite damaging:

> I think this is something we should be re-addressing as Christians, particularly in the way we talk to the 'youth' section of churches. It's totally unrealistic and in fact damaging to tell people that they should have zero sex drive or sexual feelings until the day they get a ring on their finger, and then hey presto! Engage sex drive! (but only vanilla and possibly only for procreation, and let's not enjoy it too much lest we are overcome with lust). I think we need to give people the tools to understand their sex drives, help them realise that it is God-given, and help them harness it so that they are more capable of understanding how it can at times be overwhelming, and lead us to make silly decisions when it comes to our relationships. ... I also think it's quite possible that many Christians never really get to fully enjoy sex, because they somehow can't quite shake that feeling that it's 'dirty' to enjoy sex, even if they are having it in the context of marriage. That's obviously a real shame.

Cath describes herself as 'polykinkerous', which means she engages in kink activities of a non-genital nature with other people who share the same interests. She narrates how she often engages in rope play with a transgender female, which I later explore in the section about gender blindness. Cath's main kink-based activities include nudity and rope play. She expresses her kink preferences as follows:

> I love being naked, and I love being touched (by specific people). I particularly love any kind of sensation play such as violet wands,[7] hot wax, pin wheels,[8] and the like. I adore shibari[9] and rope bondage. I like impact play such as spanking, flogging, birching, and the like. All of these types of things are kink interactions that do not necessarily involve sex. Yet I get something very intimate out of them.

For Cath, participation in BDSM does not necessarily involve genitalia, or sexual contact; Cath notes how, for her, using bondage can be 'absolutely nothing to do with any kind of sexual act'. Her participation with BDSM is 'innocent' as it is often separate from sex for her. Cath also articulates how, for her, BDSM is a form of play which is very similar to childhood play:

> Through my 'play' now, I'm regaining a sense of that childhood play again. I get to have that intimacy of touching and being touched by another person without having to see it as something sexual and bad. I don't have to worry that they are trying to manipulate me or have sex with me. We simply meet as equals, with pre-defined limits on what is not ok and safe words to use if we become unhappy with anything.

Lea Brown notes that, within her own experiences of Ds (dominant/submissive) 'play' she is able to have fun exploring her fantasies; she can use her imagination and toys to bring fantasies to life, and this in turn leads to self-discovery and personal growth. All of these elements in Ds play echo the nature of childhood play. Brown elucidates:

In my own lived experience of Ds, I have found that the power that allows me to swim deeply in *eros*, and bring healing to my body and spirit, begins with its primary nature as *play* ... there are two primary components that make play possible: our imaginations and our toys. (2010, pp. 147–8)

As already noted, for non-sexual consensual play, Cath explores this practice with people she trusts. However, because of her understanding of sex and emotions as intertwined, for Cath, the only resolution is to engage in play of a sexual nature with her husband:

I'm a sexual submissive. I like being overpowered sexually, being chased, having certain levels of fear and force applied during sex, because I find it a turn-on. Being desired to such an extent that the other person will *make* me comply to their sexual demands (that I want anyway), is fantastic. However, what I've learned is that this can be overwhelming to me emotionally. I absolutely cannot engage in this type of interaction with someone I don't have absolute trust in – and I don't just mean for my safety at the time of the interaction. I need to know that they love me during the interaction, and I need to know they are going to love me after the interaction. I need them to be able to take care of my emotional well-being, and that they won't treat me differently outside of a sexual environment because of how we have behaved during the sexual interaction. Currently, the only person I know who I trust to provide this is my husband.

Cath describes how being sexually submissive also entails being emotionally submissive, and she feels both sex and emotion cannot be separated:

Firstly, I should say that I don't separate sex and emotion. Because this is my emotional make-up, I find it difficult to understand people who are capable of strictly casual interactions. I know they exist, I just find it difficult to empathise, because I am VERY emotional, and tend to form very strong bonds with people I'm physically intimate with, though those people are very few and far between. On to the spiritual side, yes I certainly view sex as having a spiritual and mystical dimension. There is an 'extra' bond formed when I have sex with someone that I can only identify as being a spiritual bond. Therefore the character and spirit of the person I'm having sex with is something that is very important to me.

BDSM practitioner Cléo Dubois describes the relationship between dominance and submission as a '"sacred" trust of bondage' (Dubois and Queen, 1997, p. 90). On the theme of trust, Mira Zussman and Anne Pierce argue that 'without full immersion into a state of trust, a scene cannot continue as consensual play, but turns instead into torture and torment' (1998, p. 30). Indeed, there is a holy trinity of BDSM, which includes mutuality, consensuality and pleasure. These three priorities are the foundations for BDSM scripts, which can lead to further pleasure states, including healing and catharsis.

Regarding roles, it can be seen that the dominant 'top' is the effector of the wishes of the submissive 'bottom'. Liz Highleyman summarizes the paradox of the scene in the following terms:

The words 'top' and 'bottom' do not transparently describe a consensual SM interaction. It is the bottom's consent that allows the scene to go forward (even in a scene in which the bottom temporarily agrees to forego consent). The bottom controls the foundation upon which the interaction is built, while the top often controls the specific details and direction of the scene. The top's pleasure depends on the bottom's willingness to engage in the interaction. The failure to grasp this paradox underlies many of the moral arguments against erotic domination and submission. (1997, p. 155)

Cath describes the relationship between the top and bottom in a mutual, consensual and pleasurable scene as a 'flow of energy' which is 'sublimely beautiful':

I do feel that there is something inherently spiritual in some aspects of BDSM play. Submissives are often looking to deny ourselves something, in order to give something to our Dominant partner, and then we receive something back from them when we see how much pleasure we have given them. It really is a 'power exchange', where energy is flowing from one to the other and back again. It can be sublimely beautiful to be part of, or to witness. It can also be absolutely horrible to be part of or to see if something in it is warped.

As Cath is an advocate for BDSM, I was surprised to read her discussion of practices she considers 'too far'. She expresses how she finds the practice of humiliation incongruent with her Christian faith, as she states:

I certainly feel that some S and M activities go too far, and into the realms of injury that I don't believe is good from either a physical, psychological, or spiritual perspective. However, this isn't something that I've had an issue with in my personal practice. The activity I have the biggest issue with in terms of my faith is the practice of humiliation. From a spiritual and faith perspective, I believe that the way we interact with one another should be uplifting and not down-putting. I must admit that I struggle with understanding why someone would want to be humiliated.

BDSM is not boundary-less. Individuals who engage in the practice have their own boundaries, based upon individual ideas of what is appropriate or inappropriate. As a subjective practice, these boundaries depend on the practitioner, but this only serves to reinforce the importance of mutual consent in the preparation of scenes and the vital component of trust when carrying them out. The holy trinity of consensuality, mutuality and pleasure is used to benchmark the limits and boundaries for individuals involved in the practice.

Spiritual and Emotive Freedom

Of course, many of us may claim to have had, at one time or another, an SM experience so intense that we have been moved to compare it to a religious experience. But for some people, the kind of transcendental, cathartic potential of SM is perceived quite literally as part of a spiritual continuum. They really do believe that SM brings them closer to God. (Woodward, 1998, p. 7)

The links between bondage and religious experience are well documented in the literature on BDSM, and this is where Cath's story becomes a source for theology, as we explore how her experiences of BDSM connect with her experiences of the divine.

In the religious/spiritual special edition of the fetish magazine, *Skin Two*, Woodward's citation above is echoed by Julia Collings, who claims that 'pain leads to beyond pain and the universal consciousness' (1998a, p. 51). Collings states:

An SM rush is the gaining of life. It is about being reborn stronger, able to take more pain or restraint next time, after surviving the ordeal. Christian myth gives us the analogy of Christ who, dying in prolonged agony, rises from the dead three days later even more powerful than before. Each of us who indulges in an SM scene can be said to be reliving the experience of the religious hero. (1998a, p. 51)

The ritualized aspect of BDSM, from a theological perspective, is similar to both religious ritual and prayerful worship. For Cath, the parallels between bondage, meditation and prayer were connected during an episode she recalls at her prayer group within her church:

I've just started a series on prayer with my church group this past week. While we were sitting quietly listening to a piece of worship music, it suddenly occurred to me that I really wanted to be doing it whilst tied in rope. The meditation aspect of having to just 'be', and waiting on God really hit me. It really hit me that being tied in a meditative posture, having perhaps a candle to focus on and some worship music might really help with the 'be still and know that I am God' aspect of prayer! I felt a huge, physical yearning for it. Perhaps I should start a new type of prayer group!

Cath is not alone in seeing the potential of the connection between bondage, sacral space and Christian prayerfulness. Zussman and Pierce's anthropological study (1998) is a significant example of how SM practices demonstrate an affinity with ecstatic religious experiences. Collings's imagery of suffering and survival in a BDSM scene described earlier as spiritually nourishing is also echoed by Zussman and Pierce:

In S/M ritual, one can feel the extremes of physical endurance and psychic transcendence that sacred books just talk about. A crown of thorns is neither myth nor metaphor – it can be worn. A cross is something one can indeed endure. (1998, p. 16)

Collings assigns clear roles to the characters in a scene: the dominant being the divine and the submissive being the devotee. Yet, as we have previously noted through Highleyman's explanation above, roles are exchangeable within the scene: the devotee can become the divine and vice versa. Peter Sweasey offers one such example in detailing the story of Mike, a devout Catholic who describes himself as sadomasochist, '"turned on" by the crucifixion' (1997, p. 90). In articulating how he reconciles his faith with his sexuality, Mike states:

God has given me my sexuality and it's as much part of me as my belief in God. There is absolutely nothing which God cannot accept of me ... God knows all of me, including my desires, and loves them as part of me. So, no matter how sadistic or masochistic they are, they can still be beautiful, wholesome, pure, positive, life-affirming and valuable, because as a part of who I am they are being worked upon by God (Sweasey 1997, p. 91).

Although I heed Jeremy Carrette's warning that 'what sexual

theologies need to explore is how the fetish and sadomasochistic scene can contribute to a theology of bodily suffering without recourse to psychoanalytical registers' (2001, pp. 292–3), it is important to acknowledge the positive psychoanalytic implications of BDSM as a cathartic experience. Tigert observes how 'healing takes place in relationships rather than in isolation' (1999, p. 82) and it is apparent that the relationships within a BDSM scene can allow healing to occur. In addition to the pairing of roles such as dominant/submissive, divine/devotee, we also have healer/healed. Brown explores how the components of play, 'its characteristics, parameters and lived experience can contribute to a spiritual and theological understanding of its healing and liberating power' (2010, p. 141). Brown likens the healing process to giving birth: 'digging deeply into our bodies in order to let our souls howl, is not a timid act' (2010, p. 149). For Brown, liberation and healing comes from 'digging deeply into one's fears, secrets, shame, arousal, fantasies, desires, hopes, insecurities, inhibitions, strengths, needs, pasts, and present' (2010, p. 149). Like Zussman and Pierce claimed before her, 'bondage can give rise to psychic or emotive freedom' (1998, p. 23).[10] They describe how the senses are heightened because the body is restricted in bondage, and this can produce a calm and euphoric state which is often the result of being bound. This, they claim, is similar to the calmness of a baby being wrapped in swaddling, or a patient in a straight-jacket:

> For those who are sensitive or receptive to it, constriction and bondage are profoundly liberating forces. One relinquishes one's body to the care of another, and that other must be one imbued with a tremendous degree of trust. Thus, in psychological terms, one is taken back to the earliest of human psycho-social developmental stages … in which the infant struggles between trust and mistrust. (1998, p. 30)

Danielle Lindemann (2011) explores the position of 66 professional female dominatrices who consider their work with their male clients as 'sex therapy', which is 'psychologically beneficial' to clients, and they therefore consider themselves as 'therapists' (2011, p. 151). However, more pertinent to my discussion here is the work of

Corrie Hammers, who provides an example of BDSM as a positive psychoanalytical intervention, as she conceptualizes BDSM as 'somatic intervention' for the women who experience it (2014, p. 69). Her work explores the experiences of women who adopt a submissive role and thereby 'use BDSM to (re)enact their sexual trauma in an attempt to "undo" somatic dissociation' (2014, p. 69). This notion of the practice of bondage as a means for personal healing and well-being is one which counters previous entrenched considerations of BDSM as pathological, perverse, warped and damaging. Bondage is thus positioned as a positive somatic interpolation, one in which mind and body can be realigned. Hammers notes how this was not possible within traditional therapeutic contexts: 'BDSM was the necessary somatic intervention that was not possible within the talking therapies, engendering as it did the somatic refusal to ever be silenced again' (2014, p. 82). For Hammers, the body is a site for positive relational experiences with others through BDSM practices, where negotiation and consensuality are prioritized in order to obtain mutual pleasure and somatic healing. Hammers promotes somatic intervention as a means for connection, noting that for one participant: '[when] her mind and body were not connecting, and her body needed repair ... BDSM allowed the "pain to move"' (2014, p. 78). In similar terms, Cath articulates how she experiences a therapeutic release of her emotions after being in bondage. She states:

> I have a tendency to give too much out, and tend to bottle my emotions up such that they get stuck way up in my throat somewhere. When I get irritable, down on myself, depressed for no real reason, I'll often ask my husband for impact play. The act of being spanked or flogged or cropped or such like gives me permission to cry out. It's a safe way of letting all these emotions out, without fear of being judged for them. A sort of cathartic release. Very often I'm left feeling very peaceful afterwards, and more capable of sorting through thoughts that had become jumbled.

The cathartic element of release and healing is the main reason Cath engages in bondage. She describes how, although the appearance from the outside of someone in bondage can seem restrictive and abusive, internally it is wonderfully freeing:

> When I'm in rope (and other forms of bondage to a lesser extent), I feel an immense amount of freedom. It's an interesting dichotomy that something that looks from the outside to be an abusive and constricting thing can feel absolutely wonderful and freeing from the inside. I wonder sometimes whether it is the appearance of many aspects of BDSM from the outside that give it such a bad name. How something appears can be the plural opposite of the experience of it.

Hammers describes the 'aftercare' of a BDSM scene as an example of positive human relationships, 'wherein the top (the one inflicting the pain) tends to the bottom's emotional, mental and physical needs' (2014, p. 80). Cath describes her own experiences of aftercare in relation to her emotional sensitivity and well-being:

> Often, the result of being in rope bondage for me is similar to having received a massage, or having taken a yoga class. It's a healing thing. I can just let go, stop worrying about my body or my emotions, and just be. I'm frequently quite 'spaced out' when I am released from the bondage. I need to be able to sit quietly on the sofa with a blanket and watch comforting films or read a book. I will usually need to be given a warm drink and something to eat as well. If someone doesn't want to do this, I will either not play with them, or will look for someone else to be present who I trust to give me this aftercare. My emotions can at times be a little delicate, so I've learned that the company I keep during and after a rope session is very important to my emotional wellbeing.

Hammers became fully aware of her own position as researcher when she observed the emotive freedom and release of her participants. She describes how accessing BDSM space was 'a rather daunting and emotionally taxing experience' (2014, p. 76) for her; and she describes 'surface encounters' by which she got close to 'the pain and vulnerability that BDSM elicits without full immersion' (2014, p. 16). She states:

That said, not having ever experienced what BDSMers refer to as 'head space' – the high produced from the body's physiological response to intense pain and the 'loss of self' that follows – nor the sheer terror and vulnerability that comes with pain play, I fully recognize that my own (corporeal) knowledge of this world is a limited one. (2014, p. 76)

Gender 'Blindness' and the BDSM Scene

I have found that those people who are active in 'the scene' – those who attend BDSM workshops, clubs, and meet-ups are far more 'gender blind' than those who keep their interactions private and pick people up online. It's actually a very accepting scene (at least, in my local area it is). We do all come to things with our own prejudices, but people work very hard at overcoming these. I have seen on several occasions straight male dominants involved in non-sexual play such as rope play or impact play with male submissives, for example. Watching aftercare between two people who have engaged in this type of play can be very touching – a straight man does not often stroke another man's hair in comfort, for example, or wrap him up in blankets, hold him, and feed him chocolate. It is incredibly intimate and touching to behold, and I love that these gender/orientation barriers get broken down in such interactions.

The fetish scene can be a site where identities of gender and sexual orientation can queer traditional binary constructs. Cath's assertion above, describing tenderly the interactions between two heterosexual males following non-sexual rope play, enables BDSM to be located as a theological action of relationality and intimacy which overcomes the gendered norms which get in the way of homosociality and intimacy. To borrow Carrette's terms 'in the loss of self in submission to the other, or in the responsible act of dominance, we find a ritual exchange where bodily intensity and limits become pathways to intimate expressions of love' (2005, p. 25). Thus the potential to disrupt gendered normativity and enter into social relationships where bodies become both vulnerable and playful is possible.

Bauer's work (2008) unpacks the notion of BDSM as a place for exploring gender and transgressing gendered bodies, which is not always possible in mainstream culture. He notes how within BDSM communities, 'its boundaries are not necessarily restricted by its own skin' (2008, p. 248). In offering one example to exemplify this notion of transgressive genders, Bauer notes how within the dyke/trans BDSM communities 'dildos' often become 'dicks'. Bauer states that 'language is used to capture a material experience that shifts bodily boundaries' (2008, p. 242). Jacob Hale similarly sees participation in role play scenes as transgressive of gender:

> when I was a boy with my dyke daddy, in that culture of two I was a boy. I was not an adult woman playing a boy's role or playing a boy, nor was I an adult woman doing boy in some other way. Daddy's participation was necessary for me to be a boy with her. (2003, p. 65)

For Hale, the language of 'daddy' and 'boy' is used to reconfigure bodies that would otherwise be interpellated as female. Pat Califia is a transman. Before transitioning, Pat wrote *Public Sex* in 1995 while self-identifying as a lesbian and BDSM practitioner. In an example from the book written at this time, Califia provides an amusing example exploring the idea that gender is not as significant as the sexual practices one engages in. Califia said, 'if I had a choice between being shipwrecked on a desert island with a vanilla lesbian and a hot male masochist, I'd pick the boy' (1995, p. 159).

BDSM 'play' is a queer endeavour, as it subverts the traditional hegemonic understanding of the supposed connection between gender and sex and the heteronormative values of society. It exposes the parody on which gender performativity is placed. BDSM communities that suspend a gendered view of bodies allow participants to choose which gender they perform, or they can choose not to perform gender at all. Bauer states:

> A number of members of this community, such as genderqueers, have assumed gender identities that transgress the binary gender

system. While genderqueers do not identify full time as either men or women, they do not conceive of themselves as in the middle of the spectrum or as androgynous either. Their gender is rather fluid (shifting) and multiple at the same time, which means that their positioning within a variety of genders depends on the context. (2008, p. 238)

Gary Taylor and Jane Ussher's work 'Making Sense of S and M' (2001) precedes Bauer's exploration of gender as transgressive in BDSM communities. They note how the 'play' element of fetish spaces allows participants to adopt new identities. One participant in their study states:

It's more to do with the confusion of the two (male and female gender) ... like I'll talk about my cock and stuff when it's quite apparent that I'm female and I will refer to myself as he ... she ... whatever feels right ... it's more gender fuck really, it's not strongly identifying with one or the other ... it's about playing with the whole notion of gender ... (2001, p. 303)

Thus, BDSM becomes a dissident act in terms of gender conservativism. It allows a projection of genderqueer activism and politics to be developed through 'an understanding of SM as deliberately, consciously antithetical to a sexual hegemonic, namely patriarchal heterosexuality' (Taylor and Ussher, 2001, p. 302). The BDSM community provides a space for performative gender to be transcended. Zussman and Pierce note how this alternative space remains perverted, as 'perversion ... is defined as sexual gratification gained by anything other than heterosexual genital intercourse' (1998, p. 17). For Althaus-Reid, such per/versions are just different versions which counter normative understandings of sex, and she reminds us that sexual contact is not the point in BDSM scenes: 'sexual organs are excessive and therefore do not need to be biologically located' (2000a, p. 157). Althaus-Reid continues, drawing parallels between the absence of sexual organs in biblical narratives and in fetishist subcultures:

Take the story of the virginal conception. There are no sexual organs in this narrative of sexual reproduction of a human being, but rather an objectification of sexual organs in the spirit which descended upon Mary. And even then we do not know what it descended upon. (Her vagina? Her womb? Her 'heart'?) Between that and getting yourself a leather suit or high-heeled corset-laced boots and making of them the guardians of your desires, there is conceptually not much difference. The fetishist epistemology is the same. (2000a, p. 150)

Lorca Jolene Sloan (2015) has proposed that non-sexual relationships through BDSM can be formed for individuals who self-identify as asexual. Sloan argues that the expression of affection within a BDSM scene is not linked to sexual attraction or sexual expression. Her proposal is entirely congruent with the argument that BDSM is non-sexual, yet she does not discuss how BDSM practices can potentially be 'gender blind'.

Without wishing to belabour this point of BDSM as a space for transgressing normative ideas of gender and sex, Hammers concurs that BDSM practices challenge gender hierarchies and compulsory heterosexuality, as BDSM 'engenders a form of relating that moves beyond genitalia' (2014, p. 71). The discussion on spiritual and emotional freedom gained through bondage practices is also one which enables a freedom from the pain and damage caused by gender regulation on genderqueer bodies. Brandy Simula describes such a space as a 'queer utopia' in an article of the same title (2013). For Simula, the emphasis on interrelationality and interaction is more significant than the concept of gender and the power gender holds:

In these moments of ecstatic, nonsequential time, participants repeatedly describe experiencing sensations of freedom, particularly from the heteronormative and gender regulative discourses that they perceive as ubiquitous in other aspects of their lives. The absence of heteronormativity and gender regulation in these spaces allow participants to glimpse the horizon of queerness – a horizon beyond which gender and heteronormativity have ceased to regulate bodies, lives, and experiences. (2013, p. 83)

Simula describes the potential of such a queer utopia in language that is fitting with the mission of a theology of sexual stories:

Importantly, participants' resistance to gender regulation allows them to engage in both personal and community transformation by creating a social world in which alternative and non-gendered presentations of self are intelligible to others. (2013, p. 85)

Revisiting Cath's story provides first-hand examples of what she terms 'gender blindness'. Within her interactions with other non-normative individuals, she observes how they often have a heightened self-awareness and self-confidence. She says:

I have found that male submissives, cross-dressers, and trans-gendered people are among some of the most introspective and sorted individuals I've met in the scene. Generally, they are 'bucking the norm' to such an extent that they've really had to spend a lot of time figuring themselves out. They've also had such a lot of hostility and opposition both in and out of the BDSM scene that they have questioned themselves greatly, and so tend to be very certain of themselves.

Cath describes her playful non-sexual episodes with one of her most trusted partners, a transwoman, who we will call Rachel:

I have a close friend, who happens to be a M-F transgender lady, who I do shibari and some pain play with. I will usually keep my knickers on during these interactions, but we get a lot of skin-on-skin contact with one another when we play, which I adore. We both get something out of these interactions, yet neither of us fancy each other, so there is never any temptation to take it to a sexual level. I'm not sure how to explain that her putting clothes pegs on my nipples doesn't feel sexual, but somehow it doesn't! Neither is it purely 'friendly'. It's something else in between.

Beyond Bondage? Individuation and Transcendence

Althaus-Reid notes how 'stories of sexual fetishism carry many theological elements to reflect upon' (2000a, p. 151). The discussion so far has pointed to at least two identifiable outcomes emerging from the practice of BDSM that have significant contributions to make to sexual theological discourse. The first includes the healing potential achieved through prayer and meditation during bondage, which offers self-satisfaction and a feeling of wholeness. Second, the BDSM space offers freedom from traditional gender politics, allowing participants to 'switch' gender, transgress gender or transcend gender. These outcomes – spiritual and emotive freedom and a queer utopia – move the image of BDSM from its perverted shackles and imagine it as a theological resource. Indeed, 'spirituality' has often been misused as a term which is uncertain and indefinite. I agree with Paul Heelas in his statement that 'it has become a commonplace to state that the meaning of the term spirituality is "vague", "fuzzy", "obscure", or extremely "ambiguous"' (2009, p. 758). Therefore, I borrow his definition of the term, which is committed to a broad and inclusive understanding of the term:

> one of the most obvious meanings found in the discourses of spirituality has to do with life itself. It is the force, energy, or vitality that sustains us. It has to do with our natural goodness and wisdom. It is the life we are born with – basic attributes, capacities, capabilities, potentialities. Once experienced, spirituality flows through our lives to heal, to empower, and to inspire creativity and wisdom, change ill-being into well-being, enable us to become truly 'alive'. (2009, p. 759)

Jeremy Carrette and BDSM

Carrette's scholarship is significant as an example of one of the few theological engagements that does not view BDSM as a perversion. Yet he also warns that 'we need to be cautious about simplistic assertions between S&M and Christian theology' (2005, p. 15).

Facile theological parallels can be and are often drawn between Christian martyrdom and BDSM such as those posited by Mark Jordan. Jordan connects theology and BDSM within the following references: 'pursuing any of these alternatives, we will find ourselves learning that sexual sadomasochism lies close to many of our "purely religious" experiences than we might have supposed' (2002, p. 168), 'the abiding theological virtue is submission' (2002, p. 213) and 'priestly cassocks or monastic robes figure so prominently in some S&M rituals' (2002, p. 218). Similar parallels are drawn within the Jewish tradition. In Zussman's text 'Fairy Butch and the Labia Menorah' (2001), she discusses BDSM parody and play as performed within a San Francisco dungeon, concluding that such parody and play are therapeutic for those who have felt excluded and alienated from their religious roots. However, it is significant to note that such analogies do not appear to be considered simplistic or inane by the participants and observers. Yet Carrette wishes to differentiate BDSM and asceticism as two very different practices.

Carrette sees Christian asceticism as distinct from BDSM, as the latter is 'a recent discourse' (2005, p. 14) and a 'modern invention of just over 100 years old' (2005, p. 16). He views BDSM as a product of late capitalist society, rather than previously featuring as part of the Christian tradition. Although the exploitation of BDSM by capitalist enterprises can be considered a modern occurrence, Carrette does not acknowledge that, despite a shift in terminology, sadomasochistic practices and discourse both have a substantially extensive lineage within Christian history. Parallels do exist between Christian asceticism to BDSM, where pain is endured and the body is denied or punished in a quest for spiritual purity and ecstasy. Carrette fails to acknowledge that these similarities do have substance and are more than 'misplaced anachronism' (2005, p. 16). Further attention could be paid in his analysis to the pedigree and genealogy of sadomasochistic practices and discourse, as the history between Christian ascetic practices and BDSM has some overlap in relation to both the physical acts and the nature of the relationships (dominant God/submissive Christian). What is distinct in asceticism is the presence of the dominant, whose presence is felt by the spirit and mind, rather than by any physical contact.

Carrette clearly sees little value in so-called Christian sadomasochists 'bizarrely sanctioning S&M through the biblical texts on submission' (2005, p. 13). He is correct in asserting that 'it is time to move beyond the shock tactics to the careful analysis of the social order of the body politic, particularly if there is to be wider appreciation rather than alienated fears of such practices' (2005, p. 13). He notes:

> The desire to die for Christ in the literature of martyrdom, or in the bodily denial of the flesh in any form of religious asceticism, exists within a different order of experience (both socially, politically and historically) from, for example, the general practices of submission and domination in the heterosexual houses of British suburbia or the gay bathhouses of San Francisco. (2005, p. 15)

What is required, according to Carrette, is that we explore the contexts of these 'different orders of experience' (2005, p. 15). The gauntlet Carrette throws down is to ask 'what S&M subcultures ... can teach contemporary Christian theology about the importance of embodied pleasure and the material relations of our intense exchanges' (2005, p. 16), and this chapter takes up this challenge by focusing on the intimate and intense experiences of our protagonist, Cath. I acknowledge that Cath's story is in no way representative of the 'subculture'; it is just one unique narrative. Indeed, Cath's story offers further considerations which Carrette's theoretical argument does not touch upon, such as spiritual transcendence, emotive freedom, a subversion of gender (which often has a capitalist agenda in public spheres) and interrelationality. These have much to teach contemporary theology as both intimate and intense embodied experiences.

Carrette's position that BDSM can teach contemporary theology about pleasure and intimacy is further developed by two significant areas: the 'economics of relationships' and the 'dynamics of intimacy' (2005, p.17). The sexual story which is the focus of this chapter fills the gaps within his desired teaching outcomes. Cath's story, in addition to detailing both of Carrette's concerns, also looks at how the notion of play can inform theology.

On the economic front, we must heed Carrette's concerns regarding a capitalistic view of sex. The proliferation of BDSM images used in the commercial world to sell products from 'Tennent's Lager and Pot Noodle' (2005, p. 15) is one which, he warns, is too easily borrowed in simplistic discussions about BDSM and theology without an appreciation of the depth of intensity and experience of the BDSM exchange. He is concerned that BDSM has been globalized, and because of this, its non-normative, countercultural status has been diluted. Yet the practices and experiences detailed in this chapter are not watered down by globalism. I share Carrette's concerns that sex has been traditionally prostituted to capitalism as evidenced in the often expensive accoutrements produced by the sex toy industry. Yet, it is important to balance the gains by capitalism with the transformative potency of BDSM. His argument appears not to have taken into account a discussion of personal experiences of BDSM and the transformative potential of such experiences. Engagement with a practitioner, as I have done here with Cath, would have refocused his discussion. Sexual stories, such as Cath's, recognize that engagement with BDSM practices and experiences has the potential to enrich economics of relationships, through the intense interpersonal exchange which is non-gendered and non-sexual. Capitalist gain from BDSM religious experiences should be considered alongside the economic relationship gains, based on the holy trinity BDSM model of mutuality, consensuality and pleasure.

Carrette's position is characterized by a binary of BDSM as both abuse and liberation throughout, 'S&M can be both oppressive and liberating' (2005, p. 17). Indeed, Carrette oscillates between this self-imposed theoretical binary. In this, he views BDSM as both cause of the problem and its solution. His vacillating position leads to ambiguity, but by his conclusion, Carrette offers clarity in articulating the 'intense exchange' of the non-gendered, non-sexual scene as favourable. He states, 'pleasure intensity offers an exchange in terms of gifts across identity politics and non-sexual pleasures' (2005, p. 26). Carrette posits the 'intensity and intimacy' as 'the counterpoint of capitalistic sex' (2005, p. 18) and the sharing of Cath's intimate details and the intensity of her experiences serve to address this concern.

Experiencing the Divine Through BDSM

Furthermore, Carrette develops the notion of BDSM as a religious experience (2005). His notion of intense exchange is one in which 'the intensity of pleasure becomes a revelation of God' (2005, p. 25).[11] He sees God as integral to the intimate and intense exchange:

> This loving intensity is a gift of the exchange between the created order and its creator, between life and its refusal to produce and its free will to celebrate the intensities of being alive. The divine presence in acts of erotic exchange transforms them into mysterious encounters with our God-given power and our submission to God's loving power. (2005, p. 25)

Likewise, Lea Brown does not see the BDSM act as solely shared between two partners; rather, she places God into the sacred space of the scene:

> Of course, in the end, it is not only the characteristics and parameters of Ds that can lead us to a new and liberated love for God, ourselves and others; it is the act of experiencing Ds in the company of our play partners that ultimately brings us the gift of healing and wholeness ... When we experience God's love through the non-judgemental respect and care given by another in Ds play, especially in a scene where we are revealing parts of ourselves that have been labelled as 'sick' or 'perverted', we experience the unconditional love of the Divine in profound ways that have the power to turn such damaging labels into the new names of 'whole' and 'blessed'. (2010, p. 151)

BDSM is thus a vehicle for religious experience of relating to the divine, bringing about emotive transformation and spiritual transcendence. It can be both a sexual and bodily theological practice for those who identify as Christian, which draws parallels from other religious practices, such as prayer, meditation and ritual. Bodily knowledge, as Althaus-Reid points out, provides an alternative self-knowledge: 'fetishism has a way of understanding objectives and a projected eschatology which may differ from other ways of knowing' (2001b, p. 242). In a similar vein, Hammers, who does not write from a religious perspective, notes how BDSM is credited with a spiritual status:

> the BDSM encounter is, I contend, an encounter of shared intensities – a merging of bodies – but a merging anchored in the survivor's abilities to re/constitute her own bodily boundaries. Thus, we can think of BDSM as a 'merging of souls' *through individuation*. (2014, p. 88, her emphasis)

Hammers claims that BDSM is a practice which permits the development of self in relation to others.

As a sexual practice which is not necessarily genital, Taylor and Ussher (2001) note how participants use BDSM as a means of escape from everyday life. Similar to a Christian entering a church seeking to transcend quotidian experiences in search of the divine, we can acknowledge aspects of ritual and devotion within the practices of BDSM as religious experiences. Taylor and Ussher use the analogy of a physical orgasm to highlight the spiritual high experienced by SM practitioners:

> The 'high' participants described as resulting from SM without, prior to or with orgasm was also credited with near mystical significance. It was spoken of as a heightened state of consciousness or as in some way making them more astute, more enlightened or more alive. (2001, p. 305)

The notions of BDSM as sacred, transcendental and mystical could easily allow the scene to be perceived as a church. Collings and Lenius both agree that BDSM as 'church' is a viable option:

> Pervery is both sex for the soul and religion for the future. (Collings, 1998a, p. 52)

> Circuit parties serve many of the purposes that churches serve, or, in many instances, formerly served. Those who wonder where the church is headed in the twenty-first century, will find ample food for thought here. (Lenius, 2010, p. 270)

BDSM can be explained as an 'ecstatic religion' (Zussman and Pierce, 1998, p. 19). One of Zussman and Pierce's participants notes the absence of a BDSM theology: 'how do you explain something that doesn't have a theology – an ecstatic religion – it was easier to have you find out yourself' (1998, p. 19). Yet, despite the persuasive attempts of my argument for BDSM as a form of religious practice, we must not lose sight of the brutality of some practices, which not only result in bodily pain, but can result in serious injury or fatality. Zussman and Pierce warn us 'death and permanent incapacity through S/M play has occurred' (1998, p. 20). Within Christian theology, BDSM remains a marginal practice. I would argue that it is not because of the pain element and sheer brutality of some BDSM practices that fetishist encounters are marginalized. Rather, the reason they are so taboo, even unthinkable and certainly unmentionable within mainstream Christianity, is because they defy the 'good' Christian sanctioned heterosexual penile–vaginal coitus for procreation purposes.

Cath's story identifies three major outcomes from the marrying of BDSM with theology. First, The BDSM space is one which allows somatic intervention through spiritual and emotive freedom, as described above by Cath and in the emic literature. Second, the BDSM space also can be perceived as a 'queer utopia' (Simula, 2013) in which genitalia are not signifiers of gender, and gender can be transgressed or abandoned. And, third, the BDSM space allows for encounters with the divine through alternative spiritual practices, resulting in an emerging theology of BDSM.

6

Undoing Theology

This chapter opens with Alyce's creed, a self-authored statement of her belief, which offers a liminal space between traditional theology and queer theology. This is a space ripe for exploration when undoing theology. It is within this space that religious beliefs and understandings of God have been negotiated and renegotiated, as our protagonists undo their previous belief systems. The protagonists in this book demonstrate how this space is where they oscillate between an older model of their Christian beliefs and their emerging beliefs, as they come to terms with a redesigned personal spiritual landscape.

So far, I have mobilized the experience of non-normative individuals to spotlight the cumulative impact of traditional theology on individual lives. Yet, experience itself requires undoing, and within this chapter, I undo experience by problematizing it as a source for theology. Indeed, in religious terms, my protagonists' stories document the process where they have sought to undo theology and undo God. In Chapter 2, I discussed Butler's injunction of *undoing gender* (2004), alongside Vivian Namaste's call for *undoing theory* (2009). I state now that the task for theology is to undo the dominant repetitions of the Christian tradition in relation to gender, sexuality and sex in order to make it more inclusive. Moreover, *undoing theology* uncovers the temporal nature of all theologies and life events. The chapter concludes with considerations on the temporal nature of storytelling and theology, and how a sexual eschatology is part of Christian hope for non-normative theologies.

Undoing Theology: A Manifesto

Alyce's Creed

I was created in His image and likeness,
Therefore, I am beautiful.
And I say this without pride,
For His beauty does dwell inside,
Where those who deride me,
Choose not to see.

I've wasted too many years,
Shedding torrents of tears,
Living with my shame and fear,
While casting blame on my Creator.
But now I can see,
That when others criticize me,
They criticize Him for making me what I am.
And when choosing between God and man,
God is always greater.

Jesus descended into the valley where the lepers dwell,
Where they cast aside the unclean.
He did not see the ugliness that others feared,
He only saw the beauty of their souls unseen.

From Incarnation to Embodiment: Theological Insights

The three narratives contained in this book respond to Althaus-Reid's injunction to uncover 'the biographies of sexual migrants, testimonies of real lives in rebellions made of love, pleasure and suffering' (2003a, p. 8). The life stories provide fresh ideas and creative frameworks for theologizing, which bring into the open personal and sexual narratives:

That is the point of theology without underwear, made by people whose sexual misfortunes, personal or political, need to be reflected upon as part of our theological praxis. (Althaus-Reid, 2000a, p. 28)

In addition to bringing these stories out into the open, the theological insights have struck out further by documenting the instabilities of the stories that are told: stories of lives and stories of God. Before I discuss the fragility and instability of relying on experience as a theological tool, here I briefly recap my observations with regard to the theological insights gained through the narrative chapters which relate to both embodiment and subjective understandings of God. These insights summarize the transformative experience of participants, which are formed in the liminal space between traditional Christianity and Christianity from the margins, a move in which faith is informed by personal experiences.

For Alyce, the idea of the *Tranity* is used to conceptualize her self-understanding as 'neither/nor' and her future hope of self-affirmation. She sees herself as made in the image of God, thinking back from her own embodiment and incarnation to her understanding of God. Her dual embodiment as Alyce/Jerry echoes the Christological understanding of Jesus as both human and divine. In the creed above, we note how Alyce draws strength from seeing what she sees as her 'ugliness', as uniquely made by the hands of God.

Physicality was a theme in the narratives of both Caddyman to a lesser extent, and Cath to a greater degree. Caddyman narrates his journey by referencing the conflict between his sexual and spiritual self, accumulating in his preaching of the sinfulness of homosexuality and how to overcome this through his ministry. In the presentation of his life, his narrative is punctuated by emotional wrangling as he wrestles with his traditional understanding of God. He observes how his own self-acceptance results in both an emotional and physical 'healthiness', and a healthier understanding of God.

Cath's practice of BDSM draws on analogies of physical catharsis, which allows inner pain to move as she feels she draws closer to God. Her youthful experiences of dualism – the presentation of a 'good' Christian girl versus her prolific habit of masturbation – meant that she associated her sexuality with sinfulness. It was her discovery of God's grace that allowed her to change her understanding of God, as she stated: 'The God I'd known wasn't actually someone I'd liked … But the God I discovered wasn't like that at all. He was someone who loved me, who wanted me, who was voracious for me.'

The narratives presented in this book have been produced at particular junctures on the faith journey of the protagonists. The notion of non-normative gender or sexuality being a 'wound' has resurfaced within the life stories told. These stories offer a voice that speaks back to the Christian tradition, where the 'wounds' of Christianity no longer belong only to Christ, but to Christians too. Their wounds are equally worthy of theological consideration. The protagonists here, by sharing their wounds, intend not to be portrayed as victims, but as mature Christians who have successfully negotiated their beliefs and lives to a point of self-reconciliation. Their wounds serve as doors that lead the way through pain to a sense of self as whole. The notion of doors arises in Clarissa Pinkola Estes' poem '*Abre la puerta*', which translates as 'Open the door'. Estes sees pain and suffering as a door to go through which leads to wholeness: 'Your grandmother, your grandfather, / your mother, your father have died leaving a hole in your life. / Step through that hole. It is an opening. / That hole is a threshold. That hole is a door. / Abre la Puerta, open the door' (1980). Using experience as an interpretative tool for one's biography and beliefs has been the catalyst for this book, yet experience itself can be unstable, fragile and temporal.

Undoing Experience

Theologians often identify the sources of Christian theology as coming from four categories: Scripture, tradition, reason and experience (Stone and Duke, 2006, pp. 45–6). Alistair McGrath reiterates the above sources as core to Christian theology, noting that experience is rooted in our daily lives, enabling us to theologize from the 'inward and subjective world of experience, as opposed to the outward world of everyday life' (1997, p. 223). Yet in response to McGrath, Jennie Barnsley (2016) aligns theological recourse to quotidian experiences as essential to feminist theology, utilizing a 'grounding theology' approach to life-story research of trans* participants. Characteristic of Barnsley's approach is that it:

> honours all experiences, both quotidian and numinous, according the utmost importance to what the narrator says as the only resource from which to begin; other resources complement or expand upon the story but never dictate its form. (2016, p. 117)

On Experience

In Chapter 1, I detailed Yip's ethnographical studies on identity among gay Christians. Yip asked participants about questions of authority, beliefs about God and the Bible. During the interviews he used a quantitative research methodology, including asking respondents to rank, in order of importance, the four categories generally understood as core elements to Christian faith: the Bible, human reason, church authority/tradition and personal experience (Table 6.1).

Table 6.1 Yip's sources of significance among 565 LGB Christians in the UK (Yip, 2003c, p. 141, Table 11.4).

Item	Number gave item top 2 rankings	Percentage gave item top 2 rankings	Number gave item bottom 2 rankings	Percentage gave item bottom 2 rankings
Personal experience	463	81.9	102	18.1
The Bible	333	58.9	232	41.1
Human reason	303	53.6	262	46.4
Church authority	95	16.8	470	83.2

Indeed, the four sources of significance from Yip's study cannot be taken as isolated elements, as a preference for personal experience and human reason, in turn, arguably provide a frame of reference for interpreting the Bible and interrogating church authority. One of Yip's participants provides a fitting example, as Sandra notes 'it is my reasoning and my reading of the Bible, in relation to my experience, not what the church has to say' (cited Yip, 2003c, p. 140).

Yip demonstrates that individualism conquers institutionalism, and personal experiences and human reason outweigh the imposition of authority posed by the church and Bible. Tigert makes a similar observation, noting 'the movement from external authority toward personal integrity' (1999, p. 125). One of Yip's participants, Nick, states:

> I think that if church authorities say things that go against authentic experience, then there is something wrong. Then they need to be challenged. I think church authority frequently is wrong and frequently does fail to take account of the variety of experience. And, of course, the issue of sexuality is an example of that. (Nick, bisexual man, late 40s, Church of England, Yorkshire cited in Yip 2003a, p. 150)

Similarly for Susannah Cornwall, the method of interviewing intersex Christians provided a '"missing source" for theological accounts of human sex' (2015, pp. 17–18). Although her approach is to uncover what has been missing as experiential knowledge which is significant to theology, her chapter begins by examining Scripture, tradition and reason as sources for a theological understanding of the experiences of intersex people, before tackling experience. However, in utilizing and referencing the traditional building blocks of theology, Cornwall gives them stature simply by exploring them. Significantly, she suggests that 'eliding the category of experience compromises the agency and full personhood of intersex people' (2015, p. 18). Her argument must be extendible to all Christians as sexual beings.

Experience is fundamental to the radically indecent theology of Althaus-Reid, who claims how 'radical theological praxis always starts with the living experiences of people who do radical things in their lives' (2001a, p. 60). Note the grammatical distinction between the often cited 'lived experience' as a past tense, compared to the 'living experiences' preferred by Althaus-Reid. The present continuous tense is deliberate, as the process of undoing our traditionally held beliefs is continuous too. Living experiences include referencing our sexual selves, and for all Christians this serves to document the temporality of our selves. Thus, in telling sexual stories we often document our journey of experience, Althaus-Reid notes:

> The erotic story is organized as an account of a journey based on experiences of denial, suffering, confrontation and a final crisis which is resolved by 'coming out', that is, a moment of triumph by the individual. (2001a, p. 64)

Thus experience proves to be a creative, non-fixed source of faith. For Althaus-Reid, sexual experience is a deeply personal practice that serves as an internal catalyst, where reflecting from one's own sex can serve as a liberating force:

> Engaging from our own stories in an outing of structures of oppression from our own Queer perspectives may contribute to liberating Christianity from its servitude to hegemonic ways of understanding God and reality. There is more to Queer theology than sexuality, because there is more to sexuality than sex. (2001a, p. 67)

The consensus among Yip, Althaus-Reid and Cornwall is that internal rather than external sources fashion our beliefs and theology, yet these foundations are often considered problematic as personal experience and identity formation are both fluid and subjective. They are constantly being undone. My focus on experience has provided an insight into how my participants perceive that the theologies they were exposed to, or the religious background in which they were raised, were based on narrow, limited and decent parameters.

The life stories used as a source for theology in this book have prioritized and privileged experience as a major source for theology, yet queer research relies on deconstruction and undoing. In such terms, it now remains for me to leave room for experience itself to be undone, as I consider critically the scholarship of Joan Scott and Elizabeth Stuart.

Joan Scott: Enlarging the Picture and the Evidence of Experience

Within feminist critical thought, Joan Scott provides a pathway that allows us to explore the undoing of experience. Scott also makes astute observations about the power of the visibility of experience, which is pertinent to the lives of non-normative Christians. Scott observes how exploring sexualities at the margins renders them visible. This breaks silences and opens up opportunities for sexual practices:

> Numbers – massed bodies – constitute a movement and this, even if subterranean, belies enforced silences about the range and diversity of human sexual practices. Making the movement visible breaks the silence about it, challenges prevailing notions, and opens up possibilities for everyone. (1991, p. 774)

Documenting such experiences, however temporal and fragile they may be, is 'thus to render historical what has hitherto been hidden from history' (1991, p. 775). Scott terms this 'a metaphor of visibility as literal transparency' (1991, p. 775). In adopting this metaphor of visibility, she would envisage the stories collated in this book as a challenge to normative Christian history, in what she terms as

> an enlargement of the picture, a correction to oversights resulting from inaccurate or incomplete vision, and it has rested its claim to legitimacy on the authority of experience, the direct experience of others, as well as of the historian who learns to see and illuminate the lives of those others in his or her texts. (1991, p. 776)

Scott sees value in mobilizing experience to re-vision lives of the oppressed. In her view, the knowledge individuals gain through experience as a model is important in its project of 'challenging normative history' (1991, p. 776). There is a duality in her use of experience as a useful tool to render the marginalized visible because her major critique is the way in which 'experience' is often posited as 'uncontestable evidence' [sic] (1991, p. 777). In this way, taking experience as evidence 'reproduces rather than contests given ideological systems' (1991, p. 778). Scott observes how identity is a product of experience: 'it is not individuals who have experience, but subjects who are constituted through experience' (1991, p. 779). She continues:

> Talking about experience in these ways leads us to take the existence of individuals for granted (experience is something that people have) rather than to ask how conceptions of selves (of subjects and their identities) are produced. (1991, p. 782)

In other words, for Scott, social processes are at the root of our identity formations, and those social processes are disrupted by inherent political systems, namely power systems and systems of inequality. She therefore asks us to move away from considering experience, as an appropriately solid foundation in its own right, and to go beyond this to look at the social, historical and political conditions in which experience is produced and narrated. This is why the focus on the lack of fit between messy lives and the normative Christian tradition is important. Therefore, the religious background of each life story told serves as an important lens to undo theology and to view how the theological insights gained from the narratives are grounded in their alternative practices. In theological terms, such non-normative life stories expose the cumulative impact of heteronormative theology.

Elizabeth Stuart: Undoing Experience

Just as Scott's main concern is the notion of 'experience' as subjective and personal, when in reality it is polluted by historical, political and social systems which have formed part of the oppression for the marginalized, Elizabeth Stuart considers a similar starting point for queer theology. Stuart highlights her disquiet in utilizing experience as a source for theology in terms of its relationship with traditional theology.

> Queer theology, though it begins with issues of sexuality, is not really 'about' sexuality in the way that gay and lesbian theology is about sexuality. Queer theology is actually about theology. In gay and lesbian theology sexuality interrogated theology; in queer theology, theology interrogates sexuality but from a different place than modern theology has traditionally done, the place of tradition. Queer theology denies the 'truth' of sexuality and hence declares it is not stable enough to build a theology upon. (Stuart, 2003, p. 102)

Clearly, and in contrast to the theorists informing my work thus far, Stuart is not entirely happy with using sexual experience as a starting point for theology. She continues to make out her case for the problematizing of theology from experience. Below, I have bullet-pointed direct quotations from her text for ease of presentation:

- Theologies based upon experience have also been increasingly perceived as problematic by those who stand within them, as they have become aware of the fact that any attempt to firm up concepts of experience to make them sufficiently strong to bear the weight of theology necessarily involves exclusion and doing violence to the experience of others.
- There is a danger that theologies based on experience end up ... advocating a disguised form of essentialism.
- Theologies based upon experience are also difficult for those who do not share that experience to grasp or to translate in a meaningful and not reductionist way into their own theological language.
- Thus experiential theologies can often become detached from the wider Christian community and ecclesial debates.
- While they have been extremely effective in the destruction of dominant theologies, they have generally been less successful in the reconstruction of theology.

- In other words, theologies based upon experience, whether that be the experience of the universal self, or the experience of hurt, often end up virtually ceasing to be theologies at all. (Stuart, 2003, p. 62)

In response, it is important to acknowledge how Stuart's position contests theology emerging from experience alone. Previous contextual theologies have served to document an attempt to dismantle traditional heteronormative theology, which has been both dominant and troublesome for many. Butler notes how 'dismantling forms of oppression, for instance, involves a certain way of destroying what has been built badly, built in ways that are consequential in the damage they cause' (Butler in Ahmed, 2016, p. 484). Butler continues: 'to damage a damaging machine in the name of less damage, is that possible?' (Butler in Ahmed, 2016, p. 484). Stuart's concern with the destruction and reconstruction of theologies continues to work within the paradigm of traditional theology. Examples of reconstructive theologies, such as the ones emerging from the narratives presented in this book, where individuals make sense of themselves and their faith, make a much-needed contribution to theology. Yet, I tend to agree with Stuart's final point that 'experiential' theologies virtually cease to exist, and that is due to the constant rewriting and re-editing of our life stories and belief systems, which is discussed later in this chapter.

Therefore, Stuart is right in asserting that to focus on experience and one's own authority is dangerous since it risks turning God into a 'mirror-God simply reflecting our own image' (Stuart, 2003, p. 29). Althaus-Reid is equally concerned with experiential theologies becoming a God-mirror, but her position is that widening the picture to spotlight our experience corrupts socially constructed normativity. Therefore, such a reversal of positions is what highlights the instability of the grounding of grand narratives within theological traditions:

Even the God at the margins of many radical theologies has become only a lateral shadow or God-mirror. But the aim of the corruption of the ideology of normativity by sexual contamination, which informs our Queer theological path, is to move objects and subjects of theology around, turning points of reference and re-positioning bodies of knowledge and revelation in sometimes unsuitable ways. (Althaus-Reid, 2003a, p. 52)

In a later publication, Stuart concurs with Althaus-Reid's call for corruption, noting how Christianity needs to deal with the complex and messy nature of sex:

Bodies can cross boundaries, and gender and sexuality can be dissolved. Christianity is at its heart what Marcella Althaus-Reid has termed 'indecent' but it has become 'vanilla' under the reign of patriarchy and heterosexism. It needs to become obscene: instead of dealing with sexuality and gender, the ordered categories by which we are controlled and control, it needs to deal with sex in all its complexity and messiness. (2014, p. 26)

Christian theology based solely on experience empowers Christians to define faith and spirituality (and theology) on their own terms. In agreement with Stuart, I refer to her metaphor of paracletes and parrots:

The paraclete becomes the tamed parrot, repeating our own words back to us. Scripture and tradition become authorities to be suspicious of … rather than possible sites of encounter with a transcendence that lifts us to a different place where we can see things from a different angle. (2003, p. 29)

The process of undoing theology adopts the hermeneutic tool of suspicion in order to deconstruct traditional theology. Suspicion of humanistic interpretations of Scripture and humanistic legalities in relation to tradition is required to widen the scope of God's kingdom here on earth. Such suspicion does not necessarily mean an abandonment of Scripture or tradition, nor does it mean that theology becomes suspicious of God. The reflection of God among the narratives presented in this book allows God to be free.

Stories evade solitude. Through telling and hearing stories, we relate to others. In following the mission of Jesus, the Gospels recount his telling of stories illustrating moral and spiritual lessons.

Stories therefore create a space which allows new understandings and new relationships. Sharing our stories and experience allows room for our humanity within theology. It moves us from a place of silence and seclusion, to one of radical openness. Theologizing on the basis of our intimacies and sex lives points to a messy theology that twists and turns with the trauma of our sexual struggles. Such theology provides room for our humanity to meet the transcendental.

Undoing Queer Theory/Theology

It is curious that queer theory, informed as it is by poststructuralism, would lead to such experience-based work as found in this book. In this sense, queer theory has become undone by adopting it as a method to conduct experience-based work. A poststructuralist approach means that we do not seek knowledge by understanding an object, such as a text, in itself, but rather that we look at the systems of knowledge, exploring cultural products and analytical concepts that produced the text. Yet the focus on subjective experience of Christianity as a systematic backdrop to the narratives means that experience is paramount in terms of the texts produced.

In moving beyond identity politics, two aspects of Butler's consideration of gender include intelligibility and recognition, as she demonstrates how categories of gender are inadequate determiners. In *Bodies That Matter*, Butler considers individuals who inhabit those categories differently, whether that is their intention or not. Therefore, in Butlerian terms, sexual storytelling displaces the 'hegemonic symbolic of (heterosexist) sexual difference' (1993, p. 91). Furthermore, the sexual storytelling I advocate allows us to explore the stories of those who inhabit Christianity differently, which contribute to the need for recognition and the remapping of sexualities in theological terms.

In Chapter 2, I explored Guest's concerns with queer theory as an elitist discourse, far removed from the grassroots communities and lived realities of life for non-normative individuals. Stuart is equally concerned with queer as a theory but not figuring in the lives of people:

[Queer theory] is fine as a theory but where are the spaces and incentives in most of our lives to perform gender subversively? Queer theology has to address these concerns. (2003, p. 103)

Thus, theology becomes imaginative in the marrying of queer as a theory and theology with the radical agenda of undoing. Undoing enables us to deconstruct previously traditional dominant theologies. Within theology, queer theory allows for 'undoing' in Butlerian terms and is an ideal tool to document the trajectory of beliefs across a life course, recognizing that beliefs are temporal and change. The impact of our undoing is potent because we produce or attend to the dynamic vulnerability of others' life stories.

Stuart's theology is informed by her concern that repetition equals stalemate. Her contention is that 'gay and lesbian theology reached a stage of theological breakdown and this manifested itself in a tendency to simply repeat itself' (2003, p. 11). Stuart observes how queer theorists perform and repeat gender, 'with critical difference in order to subvert it' (2003, p. 11). Such critical difference rubs against normative expectations, and in theological terms, she therefore advocates critical, non-normative, repetitions in order to bring 'to birth a whole different and thoroughly theological approach to sexuality' (2003, p. 11). The theology of sexuality is far too loaded with anti-rhetoric against non-normative sexualities: there is considerable work for theologians to undo. So instead of allowing traditional theology to be repeated, undoing subverts the performativity of church and sex. This queer approach to exploring sexual theology from individual experiences is based on disruption or undoing of religion. It is important to recognize repetition with difference as a powerful daily act, just as Stuart is aware of Butler's notion that 'gender is inscribed on the body through repetition' (2003, p. 11).

Repetitions of Christian traditional understanding of sex and sexuality feature prominently in current ecclesiological concerns regarding same-sex marriage, for example. Similar repetitions on the role of women in the church have been equally at odds with the equality agenda which is now upheld in legislature. Thus the problem lies in the fact that the church has been repeating a heteronormative, vanilla, understanding of sexuality and of binary gender, without critical difference. It is the task of undoing theology to rupture these repetitions, and through this rupture, the relationship between queer theory and Christianity can be theologically transformative:

> Repetition with a critical difference is at the heart of Christian practice and therefore there is a kinship between queer and Christian and more, that Christian theology has the ability to prevent queer theory falling into repetitious nihilism. Christianity is a queer thing. (Stuart, 2003, p. 11)

The general principle of theological undoing recognizes that our belief systems are repeatedly being undone. In the next section, I note how this undoing frees God to be God-self. Within this undoing, there are parallels of Butler's repetition of gender through performativity. In similar terms, experiential and biographical theology demonstrate how religious life can be seen in terms of religious performativity: our spiritual selves are the product of religious, social and other contextual constructs. Traditionally, religious identities have been constructed through the repetition of normative understandings of Christian theology, a form of compulsory Christianity, or Christian-normativity. Undoing these traditional understandings of Christianity through a focus on radical subversion through sexual storytelling demonstrates the arbitrary foundations on which normative understandings of religion and theology are based. It is important to remember that Christian normativity does not exist solely on a theological or religious level, but it is inbuilt into society, as the normative repetitions have become mainstream and part of our cultural identities.

In keeping with the authenticity and realism which has laced these theological considerations, my undoing of theology evades providing a platform or model for sexual storytelling. If I have set up expectations for a new theological framework thus far, then as soon as it is documented here, it would rely on being undone. Theology is characterized by the language we use to talk about God, and we use language to tell stories about God. So whatever stories we tell, and whatever new theology emerges, the important conclusion is that they are fragile and temporal. The life narratives within this book demonstrate that instead of being consciously certain of who we are, where we have been and what we have learnt from these experiences, what actually happens is that we continuously redraft where we have been and what we have learnt all the time. Our lives are demarcated, not by the historical narratives we present, but by our understanding of the nomadic journeys we have made, with a few remaining tent poles to show where we have been. As part of this insight, we need to explore the function of experience as unreliable and unstable.

In light of the theological contributions made by my protagonists, theology is undone, and this points to a belief system that is based on experience which can never be rigidly fixed. Escaping fixed notions is in line with queer investigations. Theologizing from the basis of experience is therefore always temporal and subject to revision. The process of undoing theology means we renounce previously held beliefs and theology, and we undo them from within, using our own methods based on intuition, meditation and thought. The process of undoing allows us to become survivors. The biographies and theologies of sexual migrants offered in this book highlight that the changing nature of our beliefs, of our stories and of our understanding of God is fragile. Yet, this fragility makes our stories more valuable.

Within this book, the three protagonists, Alyce, Caddyman and Cath all demonstrate how their previous beliefs and assumptions have become undone. Alyce moved away from her Catholic faith which no longer would recognize her, yet she dreamed of a day when the church would welcome her. Within Caddyman's story, we note how testimonies are constantly edited and re-edited as life unfolds. Cath rejects the traditional Christianity which plagued her childhood and teenage years with feelings of shame and guilt. Undoing theology is characterized by contingency, temporality, fluidity, becoming and unbecoming as its key indicators.

The repeated undoing of our belief systems means that we are, essentially, Christian nomads. We can only ever say where we have been and where we have currently set up camp, but there is no 'home', there is no certainty, it is all in the journey. Nelle Morton's *The Journey is Home* (1986) is an influential example of personal transformation through religious understanding over a period of ten years. Morton writes: 'Maybe journey is not so much a journey ahead, or a journey into space, but a journey into presence' (1986, p. 227).

Undoing God

Just as Butler notes we are undone by one another through grief and desire, God is undone by non-normative Christians by the same emotions. We grieve normativity; we grieve the churches whose positional statements reject us; we grieve no longer belonging to traditions that bind together God's people. This is clearly highlighted in each of the narratives offered in this book. Alyce grieves her traditional Catholic faith; Caddyman grieves heteronormativity and the impact of compulsory heterosexuality on his life. He desired to be accepted, to conform, and he attempted this through the Christian sanctification of heterosexual marriage. Cath grieves how irreconcilable her sexual practice is with her church. Precisely because Cath's sexuality informs her faith, she self-identifies as a liberal Christian with a strong sense of conviction.

Yet, to focus on grief is only one aspect of the 'undoing' in Butler's thesis. We are undone by desire too. We desire an open, inclusive God, who is freeing in their creative abundance. This is why contextual theologies have been so important in allowing Christians to conceptualize a God who is welcoming, affirming and loving. Goss observes how, within traditional Christian theology, Jesus 'is penetrated by the patriarchal Roman system, nailed to the cross. His flesh is penetrated by the phallic system of patriarchal conquest and rule' (2006, p. 550). By undoing God, we allow God to be free. Traditional, normative Christian theology has resulted in a God who has been bound tightly in biblical leather and traditional ecclesiology. Yet God's consent was never sought in this fixed image which has been created throughout tradition. Althaus-Reid observes how:

Jesus has become a monopoly with strict control on spiritual production of meaning and exchange. However, at the grassroots there is always discontent with the unreality and oppressive powers of these theological meta-productions of God and Jesus. (2000a, p. 95)

Also theologizing from Latin American roots, we find in the work of Juan Luis Segundo a similar desire to undo God through a critical and creative approach to Christology. Segundo claims his theology to be 'anti-Christology' (1988, pp. 15–16). In positioning the historically ambiguous Jesus as relational to others, Segundo highlights the original and creative possibilities within Christology. Therefore, Christ is reclaimed for all non-normative Christians, with relevancy and significance for individual contexts. Christ moves beyond being the liberator to being liberated, as he is sexually deconstructed, mirroring the image of the Christian:

> Then indecent theologians may say: 'God, the Faggot; God, the Drag Queen; God, the Lesbian. God, the heterosexual woman who does not accept the constructions of ideal heterosexuality; God, the ambivalent, not easily classified sexually'. (Althaus-Reid, 2000a, p. 95)

Thus contextual expectations about God are reshaped; God is creatively unbound. Queer theology can therefore move away from God as a fixed identity, and what emerges is a truly queer God: unfixed, uncapturable and unpredictable. The point of engaging in sexual storytelling is to see the possibilities of imagining God alternatively on an individual and subjective level. God is freed from bondage and is no longer cemented into a rigid theological frame. It allows us to peek through the blinds and binds to offer a wider, more creative understanding of God in the lives of individual Christians.

Yet, this is more than voyeuristic theology, as the religious, political and cultural are deeply entwined. Robert Simpson's article seeks to remind the church of the importance of sexual stories, and he compares working in the fashion industry to being a member of the church: 'The Church's own brand of sackcloth sexual theology might just be too uncomfortable for those who prefer more relaxed fabrics that feel good against the skin' (2005, p. 99). He uses the motif of a 'theological catwalk' to envisage the person of Jesus through the lens of sexual stories. Simpson reminds us of the relational power of sharing sexual stories, in theological terms:

> It has resulted in suffering, depression, and experiences of identity crisis as persons are unable to speak about who they really are, and ultimately it has distorted individual relationships with God. If people cannot honestly incorporate the sexual aspect of their lives into their experiences of the divine, then how can they possibly hope to live with integrity and in right-relation with others? (2005, p. 99)

Returning to the work of Ken Plummer is helpful here, as he notes how the sexual story provides a bridge between the individual and the community:

> the telling of sexual stories can ultimately move beyond the life of a person or community ... not only do stories work pragmatically for the people who tell them, so too they feed into and perform major tasks for societies and groups within them. (1995, p. 174)

Plummer notes how stories 'help organize the flow of interaction, binding together or disrupting the relation of self to other and community' (1995, p. 174). Although he works outside of religious frameworks, his reference allows us to see how theologically potent it is to undo God and share this with one's community. Plummer actually offers religious terminology, in the form of viewing the sexual story as a form of transcendence:

> the story may be told as a form of transcendence: the story is a means of breaking beyond ... they do not return to ritualised, conventionalised, habitualised forms of storytelling: instead they seek to break asunder, to challenge dominant narratives, to be a threat. Such stories harbour change. (1995, p. 175)

Sexual stories form part of a creative theological re-education. They work at the intersections of the individual and community, the individual and God. Throughout this book, we see how the narrators' stories negotiate individual changes in response to the cumulative impact traditional theology has had on their lives.

The fact that stories harbour change, as observed by Plummer, means that stories demarcate our understanding and interpretations of specific moments within our lives, yet our interpretations change. Storytelling thus is an ongoing affair, which results in the temporality of each story produced:

> I have slowly come to believe that no stories are true for all time and space: we invent our stories with a passion, they are momentarily true, we may cling to them, they may become our lives and we may move on. Clinging to the story, changing the story, reworking it, denying it. But somewhere behind all this storytelling there are real active embodied, impassioned lives. (Plummer, 1995, p. 170)

We cling to our beliefs; we change them; we rework them. If Christology is the story of God, then we must acknowledge that whatever contextual Gods we imagine to match our identities, cultures or situations, they will pass.

Temporality of Theology

> So much Christian theology is conducted not in the present but in the company of the past. This is particularly evident in Christian sexual discourse, which tends to revolve around trying to find a way of reconciling contemporary understandings of sexuality and gender with the tradition. No one has yet attempted to do sexual theology from an eschatological perspective. A Trinitarian model of theology done in the present in the company of past and future is desperately needed in our churches because without it liberating praxis is impossible. (Stuart, 1997b, pp. 195–6)

Since writing in 1997, Stuart's call for a sexual theology from an eschatological perspective has seen seeds begin to sprout in the work of Susannah Cornwall. Before considering Cornwall's 'sexchatology' in the next section, here I work within the remit of massaging the tension between the present and the past, by looking at the interpretative lenses through which the narratives of this book have been produced.

Each of the narratives offered are narrated through a present, interpretative lens, thereby demonstrating a present understanding of past events. When updating a life story, it inevitably undergoes a process of editing in which some sections will remain more faithful to the true events of life and faith, whereas others will be adapted through hindsight. The construction and reconstruction of biographies and life narratives as well as revising statements of belief have been a key feature of the lives of all the protagonists. Alyce has two life stories, hers and Jerry's; Cath traces the trajectory of her former traditional conservative Christian beliefs to her relaxed, liberal position today; and Caddyman's religious understanding of sexuality has reversed. He comments:

> I've also changed a lot of my spiritual convictions and references. The newer story also reflects those changes. I'm no longer speaking in terms of a religious dynamic, but rather a faith dynamic. Faith for me is much more of a broad life experience rather than a religious practice. God to me is much bigger and fuller than just a 'person of God' as in a Creator, or a Savior. God today is bigger than any creation in terms of who God is. I haven't a clue if God is a literal being, or something far different than what we may understand or relate to.

Retelling the story through a present lens requires the narrator to update the story in light of revised beliefs and revise previous beliefs that are no longer upheld. Despite the fact that all three life stories were narrated chronologically, Paul Ricoeur reminds us that a narrative is created by an individual by 'reading the end into the beginning and the beginning into the end' (1980, p. 183). In brief, we live life forwards but understand it backwards. This occurs in equal measure to the construction of statements of belief. Our narratives and theologies are constructed with a post hoc treatment; how we make sense and construct these narratives and beliefs is therefore temporal. New knowledge and fresh understandings blur the memory of the past. Liz Stanley points to this in her discussion of the 'autobiographical past':

The self who writes has no more direct and unproblematic access to the 'self who was' than does the reader; and anyway 'the autobiographical past' is actually peopled by a succession of selves as the writer grows, develops and changes. (1992, p. 61)

In light of this, with each telling of a life story and profession of belief, we observe that each story is temporal. Episodes of life are edited or omitted depending on what life experiences the narrator wishes to employ. Therefore theologies, as well as one's spiritual life, change and evolve. Within the construction of narrative, it is the lens that views the past which changes, as interpretations of the past change.

Stuart's call for a Trinity of time frames, detailed in the quotation at the beginning of this section, serves to connect with personal theologies and is grounded in the work of Paul Ricoeur. Ricoeur states that 'narrativity and temporality are closely related' (1980, p. 169) pointing to such temporality as the unity of different time frames: 'temporality consists in the deep unity of future, past, and present' (1980, p. 180). So although life events can be organized neatly into episodes, the self-understanding and interpretation of life events is organic, fluid, temporal. Steph Lawler problematizes the self-interpretation of events through memory:

In narrating a story, social actors ... draw on memories. But, not only do they interpret those memories, the memories *themselves* are interpretations. It is not simply that memory is unreliable (although it is): the point is that memories are themselves social products. What we remember depends on the social context. (2014, p. 30)

The temporality of narrative and theology signifies that subjective theologies are built on unstable foundations. Therefore, the queer methods of undoing experience, discussed in this chapter, are the ideal approach to highlight the instability of identity categories and identity markers.

The temporality of theology exists contingently in a present moment. Theology has traditionally been cognized as having the force of firm foundations, which are grounded in past traditions and present repetitions. So in Butler's terms, there is an apparent stability within Christianity, as we note it is grounded only in its repetitions that congeal to give the *impression* of continued history with a grounded origin. In one example, we observe how the repeated statements of the churches in relation to homosexuality are like a nervous stammer as the churches attempt to bolster the storm of individualization which shakes their foundations. Therefore, personal narratives are revealed in hindsight and are subject to revision, and so is theology. Traditional Christian theology is not the stable foundation we once thought but is contingent on everyone continuing to bolster its foundations. As church attendance decreases and people move away from the practice of Christian faith, its hold is threatened.[12] My participant narratives have taught us that theology is subject to revision because they evaluate received theologies from their experiential positions; they resist some parts of it; and they contribute important, new ideas. Sexual storytelling prompts us to think more flexibly, bringing new images and representations of God.

Writing from a non-religious space, Gayle Rubin observes how 'history makes fools of us' (2009, p. 371). She notes how there is 'an expectation that ... generative and world-shattering moments are supposed to be permanent conditions' (2009, p. 370). This present expectation is rooted in the past but points to the future, as it borrows from Christian understandings of futurity:

> Various forms of power, as they develop historically and in particular social contexts, animate certain movements, persons, practices, places and things with sensibilities of resistance, rebellion or transgression. But these are generally transient. Some sites of resistance are more durable or recurrent than others, but most change eventually, as the social structures of domination shift and develop ... This expectation of a final perfectibility owes a good deal as well to millennial Christianity, and its watchful expectation of an imminent return to a heavenly version in the garden of Eden. (2009, p. 370)

Stuart's theory of a theological Trinity that interconnects past, present and future time frames can be found in my consideration of sexual theology and eschatology.

Sexual Theology and Eschatology

As a branch of traditional Christian theology, a normative consideration of eschatology does not befit the exploration of non-normative lives which has been the driving force of this work. Yet, an essay by Sarah Coakley (2000) recognizes the relationship between the eschatological body and queer theory, in which the act of subversion of normative gender as a present tense activity has its ultimate outcome in utopian futures. In her Butlerian reading of the eschaton, Coakley argues how the troubling of gender by subverting repetitions of binary understandings of male/female are actions which occur in the present, but 'have their final goal in the future: they create the future by enacting its possibilities' (2000, p. 64). In this queer theorized reading of eschatology, Coakley cites Butler's notions of how we are undone by one another, through desire and grief, as 'the remaining marks of a body longing for transformation into the divine' (2000, p. 64). The postmodern body in its present form is not only a subject of numerous social constructions, she argues, but there is 'a seemingly unambiguous focus for longings, myths and quasi-religious hopes' (2000, p. 62). It is therefore this view, she concludes, which points to

> an eschatological horizon which will give mortal flesh final significance, a horizon in which the restless, fluid post-modern 'body' can find some sense of completion without losing its mystery, without succumbing to 'appropriate' or restrictive gender roles. (2000, p. 70)

Christian thought, doctrine and belief have always contained the promise of a more fulfilled life through God. Through their beliefs and practices, Christians partake in the desire to transform, with a present transformation and a future hope of being a new creation, as promised within the Pauline scriptural texts. This is a realized eschatological viewpoint. For non-normative Christians especially, the theology of eschatology has a particular future promise of abundant acceptance, free from radical vulnerability. Yet this point to the future involves a present activity, as Andy Buechel notes:

> all statements about the beyond are primarily statements about us today, full of our hopes, our concerns, and fears; they involve projections and heuristics in order to think them through. (2015, p. 99)

In considering eschatology in sexual terms, Elizabeth Stuart's work on ecclesial bodies is significant. She states that gender and sexuality are erased and therefore fade into insignificance when we take on that eschatological identity. Markers of human identity no longer matter; the binary matrices are destroyed. Stuart observes how 'identities will pass away':

> Gender, race, sexual orientation, family, nationality and all other culturally constructed identities will not survive the grave. They will pass away, the 'I' that is left, the I am that I am is not, as the popular song would have it, 'my own special creation' nor the creation of human communities, the I am that I am is God's own special creation and that is my only grounds for hope. (2007, p. 74)

Echoing Butler, Stuart argues that such eschatological erasure 'parodies and subverts all culturally constructed identities' (2007, p. 74). Not only does eschatological theology erase scars of human identities and heal wounds of those who bore non-normative identities, it serves to undo such identities.

Recognizing that a traditional understanding of eschatology has resemblances to queer theory has some ultimate grounding in both the theorization and practical elements of this book. Indeed, the eschaton in itself undoes Christianity on earth; it is still a fluid notion. The eschaton us unknowable, indescribable. It is both a Christian and queer 'becoming', it is a not-yet graspable continuum. All Christians are undone by the eschaton, as Christian eschatology is demarcated by both desire and grief. The already/not-yet paradigm of the eschaton signifies how Christians place their hopes and desires into infinite fulfilment (the not-yet), while the (already) present state of fears is grieved. We await the 'ultimacy of our sexualities in light of the resurrection' (Buechel, 2015, p. 116).

In a similar vein, Cornwall (2013a) marries this Christian doctrine to the experience of sexuality. She coins the term 'sexchatology' to define the full integration of self and spiritual identities, which has been a difficult task as documented by my participants. I offer her definition of 'sexchatology' in full in order to focus on the transcendental hope for transformation within Christianity:

> This means affirming two things simultaneously: first, that all Christian thought and theologising about sexuality takes place in the context of a present and future hope for a new creation; and second, that this new creation is to be understood not as one in which sexuality has been erased or transcended, but one in which it's become so fully and rightly integrated into human beings that it is no longer a site of pain, tragedy, violence, jealousy, doubt, shame and self-loathing as it sometimes is in the present world. (2013a, p. 155)

Beyond Our Stories

My queering of experience does not seek to deny the importance of the experiences and life stories and the radical vulnerability one places in sharing their story. Nor does it suggest that experience is not significant theologically. On the contrary, it exposes experience as a temporal condition by which we demarcate significant life episodes which contribute to our present understanding of ourselves. The temporality of theology destabilizes what is commonly understood as a religion with traditional, historical, solid foundations, which are only dominant in that they continue to be repeated. The contribution that sexual storytelling makes to the emergence of more liberal Christian attitudes threatens traditional theological discourse, more explicitly exemplified in the ongoing contemporary debates around same-sex marriages. Storytelling, whether on an individual or grand narrative scale, blends fact with fiction:

Are people fictions? We mostly understand ourselves through an endless series of stories told to ourselves by ourselves and others. The so-called facts of our individual worlds are highly coloured and arbitrary, facts that fit whatever fiction we have chosen to believe in. It is necessary to have a story, an alibi that gets us through the day. (Winterson, 1995, p. 59)

Winterson's question above can be directed towards each of the narratives offered in this book. In starting this project, I acknowledged that life-story research did not produce solid 'data' or facts, but, to borrow Winterson's term, they are 'highly coloured' and allow for us to be creative in exploring faith in untraditional terms. I did not seek to collate 'true stories' but stories that are built on our self-understandings and interpretations which we choose to present. After all, identities and Christianity are performative too.

In an interview with Judith Butler, Sara Ahmed acknowledges how the reception of texts vary according to their contexts, she states 'I like the idea that texts have lives other than the ones we give them as writers, and that these lives are partly about how texts are "picked up"' (2016, p. 482). Butler replied that 'textual evidence is not exactly data. And we end up interpreting it again' (2016, p. 482). Within the interview, Butler explores how even the subjective self becomes 'disturbingly generative' (2016, p. 484) and, with regard to this book, this works on two levels: (1) the production of further stories and (2) the participation of others in attending to the stories produced. These stories now have lives in their new existence in the general consciousness of you, the reader.

It is necessary therefore to be conscious of the space in which we transition from our previous understandings and interpretations of ourselves and those of our emerging selves. Therefore, the narratives offered in this book provide a liminal space in which our internal working selves are made and unmade. It must be said that this is a difficult journey to make. Regarding our belief systems, we often fluctuate between previous and new understandings of God and Christianity, because we need to engage with our past selves precisely to wrestle and undo them. Butler is aware of the emotional toll which is a consequence as we start 'to deviate ... from that more obedient sense of repetition' (2016, p. 484). She continues:

Deviation brings with it anxiety, fear, and a sense of thrill, and that when it is undertaken in concert with others, it is also the beginning of new forms of solidarity that make it possible to risk a new sense of being a subject. (2016, p. 484)

The thrill should not be read as an always happy ending to the fear and anxiety that precedes it. Butler evokes how the emotion of 'vulnerability can be the condition of responsiveness' (2016, p. 485). She warns how deviation can result in uncertain consequences: 'even if you are willing to those consequences, even if they can be thrilling, it can be frightening, not knowing where you are going to end up' (2016, p. 486).

Theological Troublemakers

Returning to Butler one final time, the title of her treatise on gender, *Gender Trouble*, denotes the rebellious nature of the act of causing trouble:

To make trouble was, within the reigning discourse of my childhood, something one should never do, precisely because that would get one in trouble. The rebellion and its reprimand seemed to be caught up in the same terms, a phenomenon that gave rise into my first critical insight into the subtle ruse of power: the prevailing law threatened one with trouble, even put one in trouble, all to keep out of trouble. (1991, p. vii)

Ahmed notes how 'trouble becomes a technique' (2016, p. 2), as it contests the status quo. Translating trouble theologically, we recognize that theology is temporal, observing how certain normative theologies have become the ones that get repeated ad infinitum and thus remain dominant in theological discourse. Such traditional theological repetitions remain problematic. The three stories offered within this book serve as examples of theological trouble, problematizing dominant, normative Christian theology by exposing the unfixed foundations on which traditional Christian theology has been built:

Such sexual theologies will prepare queer Christians ... to become theological troublemakers or prophets that will shake the theological roots of other Christian communities and challenge them to undertake a more inclusive theology of sexuality and justice-based sexual theology. (Goss in Gill, 1998, p. 199)

References

Ahmed, S. and Butler, J. (2016), 'Interview with Judith Butler'. *Sexualities* 19(4), pp. 482–92.

Althaus-Reid, M. (2000a), *Indecent Theology*. London: Routledge.

Althaus-Reid, M. (2000b), 'Indecent Exposures', in L. Isherwood (ed.), *The Good News of the Body*. Sheffield: Sheffield Academic Press, pp. 205–22.

Althaus-Reid, M. (2001a), 'Outing Theology: Thinking Christianity out of the Church Closet'. *Feminist Theology* 9, pp. 57–67.

Althaus-Reid, M. (2001b), 'Sexual Salvation: The Theological Grammar of Voyeurism and Permutations'. *Literature and Theology* 15(3), pp. 241–8.

Althaus-Reid, M. (2003a), *The Queer God*. London: Routledge.

Althaus-Reid, M. (2003b), 'On Non-Docility and Indecent Theologians: A Response to the Panel for Indecent Theology'. *Feminist Theology* 11(2), pp. 182–9.

Althaus-Reid, M. (2004a), *From Feminist to Indecent Theology*. London: SCM Press.

Althaus-Reid, M. (2004b), 'Queer I Stand: Lifting the Skirts of God', in M. Althaus-Reid and L. Isherwood (eds), *The Sexual Theologian*. London: Continuum, pp. 99–109.

Althaus-Reid, M. and Isherwood, L. (eds) (2004), *The Sexual Theologian*. London: Continuum.

Althaus-Reid, M. and Isherwood, L. (2007a), 'Thinking Theology and Queer Theory'. *Feminist Theology* 15(3), pp. 302–14.

Althaus-Reid, M. and Isherwood, L. (eds) (2007b), *Controversies in Feminist Theology*. London: SCM Press.

Althaus-Reid, M. and Isherwood, L. (eds) (2008), *Controversies in Body Theology*. London: SCM Press.

Alvesson, M. and Sköldberg, K. (2009), *Reflexive Methodology:*

New Vistas for Qualitative Research. London: Sage.

Anderson, T. (2001), 'Sigmund Freud's Life and Work'. *The Annual of Psychoanalysis* 29, pp. 9–34.

Ashford, C. (2009), 'Queer Theory, Cyber-ethnographies and Researching Online Sex Environments'. *Information and Communications Technology Law* 18(3), pp. 297–314.

Bacon, H. (2009), *What's Right with the Trinity? Conversations in Feminist Theology.* Aldershot: Ashgate.

Bacon, H. (2012), 'Thinking the Trinity as Resource for Feminist Theology Today'. *Crosscurrents* 62(4), pp. 442–64.

Bargh, J. A., McKenna, K. Y. A., and Fitzsimons, G. M. (2002), 'Can You See the Real Me? Activation and Expression of the "True Self" on the Internet'. *Journal of Social Issues* 58, pp. 33–48.

Barnsley, J. (2013), Grounding Theology in Quotidian Experiences of Complex Gender: A Feminist Approach. Unpublished PhD thesis. University of Birmingham.

Barnsley, J. (2016), 'Grounded Theology: Adopting and Adapting Qualitative Research Methods for Feminist Theological Enquiry'. *Feminist Theology* 24(2), pp. 109–24.

Bauer, R. (2008), 'Transgressive and Transformative Gendered Sexual Practices and White Privileges: The Case of the Dyke/Trans BDSM Communities'. *Women's Studies Quarterly* 36 (3–4), pp. 233–53.

Bauer, R. (2014), *Queer BDSM Intimacies: Critical Consent and Pushing Boundaries.* London: Palgrave Macmillan.

Bean, J. (2001), 'The Spiritual Dimension of Bondage', in Thomson, M. (ed.), *Leather Folk: Radical Sex, People, Politics and Practice.* Los Angeles: Alyson Books, pp. 257–66.

Beattie, T. (2007), Review of *From Feminist Theology to Indecent Theology,* by Marcella Althaus-Reid. *International Journal of Systematic Theology* 9(4), pp. 469–71.

Boer, R. (2010), 'Too Many Dicks at the Writing Desk, or How to Organize a Prophetic Sausage-Fest'. *Theology and Sexuality* 16, pp. 95–108.

Boisen, A. T. (1936), *Exploration of the Inner World: A Study of Mental Disorder and Religious Experience.* New York: Willett Clark and Company.

Bons-Storm, R. (2013), 'Being in Touch' in R. R. Ganzevoort, R.

Brouwer and B. Miller-McLemore (eds), *City of Desires – A Place for God? Practical Theological Perspectives.* Zürich: Lit Verlag, pp. 63–70.

Bourdieu, P. (1999), 'Understanding', in P. Bourdieu (ed.), *The Weight of the World: Social Suffering in Contemporary Society.* London: Polity Press, pp. 607–27.

Brown, L. D. (2010), 'Dancing in the *Eros* of Domination and Submission within SM', in L. Isherwood and M. Jordan (eds) (2010), *Dancing Theology in Fetish Boots.* London: Canterbury Press, pp. 141–52.

Browne, K. and Nash, C. (2010), *Queer Methods and Methodologies.* London: Ashgate.

Buechel, A. (2015), *That We Might Become God: The Queerness of Creedal Christianity.* Eugene, OR: Cascade Books.

Bullough, R. V. and Pinnegar, S. (2001), 'Guidelines for Quality in Autobiographical Forms of Self-Study Research'. *Educational Researcher* 30, pp. 13–21.

Butler, J. (1990), *Gender Trouble.* London: Routledge. Routledge Classics [2006 print].

Butler, J. (1991), 'Imitation and Gender Insubordination', in D. Fuss (ed.), *Inside/Out: Lesbian Theories. Gay Theories.* London: Routledge, pp. 13–31.

Butler, J. (1993), *Bodies That Matter.* London: Routledge.

Butler, J. (2004), *Undoing Gender.* London: Routledge.

Cahill, L. (1979), Review of *Embodiment: An Approach to Sexuality and Christian Theology* by James Nelson. *The Journal of Religion* 59(4), pp. 490–2.

Califia, P. (1995), *Public Sex: Culture of Radical Sex.* San Francisco: Cleis Press.

Campbell-Reid, E. R. and Scharen, C. (2013), 'Ethnography on Holy Ground: How Qualitative Interviewing is Practical Theology Work'. *International Journal of Practical Theology* 17(2), pp. 232–59.

Carrette, J. (2001), 'Radical Heterodoxy and the Indecent Proposal of Erotic Theology: Critical Groundwork for Sexual Theologies'. *Literature and theology* 15(3), pp. 286–98.

Carrette, J. (2005), 'Intense Exchange: Sadomasochism, Theology and the Politics of Late Capitalism'. *Theology and Sexuality* 11, pp. 11–30.

Cass, V. C. (1979), 'Homosexual Identity Formation: A Theoretical Model'. *Journal of Homosexuality* 4, pp. 219–35.

Church of England (1991), *Issues in Human Sexuality: A Statement by the House of Bishops*. London: Church House Publishing.

Church of England (1998), *Lambeth Conference on Human Sexuality*. Available from http://www.anglicancommunion.org/resources/document-library/lambeth-conference/1998/section-i-called-to-full-humanity/section-i10-human-sexuality?author=Lambeth+Conferenceandsubject=Human+sexualityandyear=1998 (accessed 30 April 2016).

Clark, J. M. (1989), *A Place to Start: Towards an Unapologetic Gay Liberation Theology*. Stirling: Monument Press.

Clark, J. M. (1997), *Defying the Darkness: Gay Theology in the Shadows*. Cleveland: Pilgrim Press.

Coakley, S. (2000), 'The Eschatological Body: Gender, Transformation and God'. *Modern Theology* 16(1), pp. 61–72.

Coakley, S. (2002), *Powers and Submissions: Spirituality, Philosophy and Gender*. Oxford: Blackwell.

Coakley, S. (2003), 'Living into the Mystery of the Holy Trinity: The Trinity, Prayer, and Sexuality', in J. M. Soskice and D. Lipton (eds), *Feminism and Theology*, Oxford: Oxford University Press, pp. 258–67.

Coakley, S. (2013), *God, Sexuality and the Self: An Essay 'On the Trinity'*. Cambridge: Cambridge University Press.

Collings, J. (1998a), 'Closer to God'. *Skin Two* 27 (Autumn), pp. 49–52.

Collings, J. (1998b), 'Once a Catholic'. *Skin Two* 27 (Autumn), p. 65.

Comstock, G. D. (1993), *Gay Theology Without Apology*. Cleveland: Pilgrim Press.

Comstock, G. D. (1996), *Unrepentant, Self-Affirming, Practicing*. New York: Continuum.

Congregation for the Doctrine of the Faith (1986), 'Letter to the Bishops of the Catholic Church on the Pastoral Care of Homosexual Persons'. Available from http://www.vatican.va/roman_curia/congregations/cfaith/documents/rc_con_cfaith_doc_19861001_homosexual-persons_en.html (accessed 30 April 2016).

Congregation for the Doctrine of the Faith (2003),

REFERENCES

'Considerations Regarding Proposals to Give Legal Recognition to Unions between Homosexual Persons'. Available from http://www.vatican.va/roman_curia/congregations/cfaith/documents/rc_con_cfaith_doc_20030731_homosexual-unions_en.html (accessed 30 April 2016).

Cornwall, S. (2010a), *Sex and Uncertainty in the Body of Christ*. London: Equinox.

Cornwall, S. (2010b), 'Stranger in Our Midst: The Becoming of the Queer God in the Theology of Marcella Althaus-Reid', in L. Isherwood and M. Jordan (eds), *Dancing Theology in Fetish Boots*. London: Canterbury Press, pp. 95–112.

Cornwall, S. (2011), *Controversies in Queer Theology*. London: SCM Press.

Cornwall, S. (2013a), *Theology and Sexuality*. London: SCM Press.

Cornwall, S. (2013b), 'British Intersex Christians' Accounts of Intersex Identity, Christian Identity and Church Experience'. *Practical Theology* 6(2), pp. 220–36.

Cornwall, S. (2014), 'Telling Stories about Intersex and Christianity: Saying Too Much or Not Saying Enough?' *Theology* 117(1), pp. 24–33.

Cornwall, S. (ed.) (2015), *Intersex, Theology and the Bible: Troubling Bodies in Church, Text and Society*. New York: Palgrave Macmillan.

Correll, S. (1995), 'The Ethnography of an Electronic Bar: The Lesbian Café'. *Journal of Contemporary Ethnography* 24, pp. 270–98.

Coventry, M. (1999), 'Finding the Words', in A. D. Dreger (ed.), *Intersex in the Age of Ethics*. Hagerstown: University Publishing Group. pp. 71–8.

Crew, L. (1991), *A Book of Revelations: Lesbian and Gay Episcopalians Tell Their Own Stories*. Washington, DC: Integrity.

Culbertson, P. and Krondorfer, B. (2005), 'Men's Studies in Religion', in L. Jones (ed.), *Encyclopedia of Religion*. Detroit: Macmillan Reference, pp. 5861–6.

Daly, M. (1985), *Beyond God the Father: Toward a Philosophy of Women's Liberation*. Boston: Beacon Press.

Daniluk, J. C. and Browne, N. (2008), 'Traditional Religious Doctrine and Women's Sexuality'. *Women and Therapy* 31(1), pp.

129–49.

Davis, J. (2010), 'Architecture of the Personal Interactive Homepage: Constructing the Self through MySpace'. *New Media and Society* 12(7), pp. 1103–19.

Deleuze, G. and Guattari, F. (1994), *What is Philosophy?* Translated by J. Tomlinson and G. Birchill. New York: Columbia University Press.

Deleuze, G. and Guattari, F. (1999), *A Thousand Plateaus: Capitalism and Schizophrenia.* Translated by B. Massumi. London: The Athlone Press.

Deleuze, G. and Guattari, F. (2000), *Anti-Oedipus: Capitalism and Schizophrenia.* Translated by R. Hurley, M. Seem and H. Lane. Minneapolis: The University of Minnesota Press.

Denzin, N. K. (2004), 'The Art and Politics of Interpretation', in S. N. Hesse-Biber and P. Leavy (eds), *Approaches to Qualitative Research: A Reader on Theory and Practice.* Oxford: Oxford University Press, pp. 447–72.

Dubois, C. and Queen, C. (1997), 'Cleo Dubois Interview', in P. Califia and D. Campbell (eds), *Bitch Goddess.* San Francisco: Greenery Press. pp. 85–96.

Erzen, T. (2006), *Straight to Jesus: Sexual and Christian Conversions in the Ex-gay Movement.* Berkeley: University of California Press.

Escoffier, J. (1990), 'Inside the Ivory Closet: The Challenges Facing Lesbian and Gay Studies'. *Out/Look: National Lesbian and Gay Quarterly* 10, pp. 40–8.

Estes, C. P. (1980), '¡Abre La Puerta! Open the Door!'. Available at http://www.herbcraft.org/estes.html (accessed 3 December 2017).

Ford, M. (2004), *Disclosures: Conversions Gay and Spiritual.* London: Darton, Longman and Todd.

Fortunato, J. E. (1982), *Embracing the Exile: Healing Journeys of Gay Christians.* San Francisco: Harper and Row.

Fulkerson, M. M. (2007), *Places of Redemption: Theology for a Wordly Church.* Oxford: Oxford University Press.

Fuss, D. (1991), *Inside/Out: Lesbian Theories, Gay Theories.* London: Routledge.

Ganzevoort, R. R. (1993), 'Investigating Life Stories'. *Journal of Psychology and Theology* 21(4), pp. 277–87.

Ganzevoort, R. R. (1998a), 'Religious Coping Reconsidered, Part

One: An Integrated Approach'. *Journal of Psychology and Theology* 26(3), pp. 260–75.

Ganzevoort, R. R. (1998b), 'Religious Coping Reconsidered, Part Two: A Narrative Reformulation'. *Journal of Psychology and Theology* 26(3), pp. 276–86.

Ganzevoort, R. R. (2001), 'Religion in Re-writing the Story: Case Study of a Sexually Abused Man'. *International Journal for the Psychology of Religion* 11(2), pp. 45–62.

Ganzevoort, R. R. (2002), 'WYSIWYG. Social Construction in Practical Theological Epistemology'. *Journal of Empirical Theology* 15(2), pp. 34–42.

Ganzevoort, R. R. (2008), 'Scars and Stigmata. Trauma, Identity, and Theology'. *Practical Theology* 1(1), pp. 19–31.

Ganzevoort, R. R. (2011a), 'Missing Men: The Ambiguous Success of Gender Studies in Practical Theology'. A Paper for the Expert Meeting *Gender Studies in Theology and Religion: A Success-Story?* Groningen, 27–28 January 2011.

Ganzevoort, R. R. (2011b), 'Narrative Approaches', in B. Miller-McLemore (ed.), *The Wiley-Blackwell Companion to Practical Theology*. Chichester: Wiley-Blackwell, pp. 214–23.

Geertz, C. (1995), *After the Fact: Two Countries, Four Decades, One Anthropologist*. Cambridge, MA: Harvard University Press.

Gelfer, J. (2009), *Numen, Old Men: Contemporary Masculine Spiritualities and the Problem of Patriarchy*. London: Equinox.

Gherardi, S. and Turner, B. (1987), 'Real Men Don't Collect Soft Data'. Quaderni del dipartimento di Politica Sociale 13, Università degli Studi di Trento. Available from http://eprints.biblio.unitn.it/4319/.

Gill, S. (ed.) (1998), *The Lesbian and Gay Christian Movement: Campaigning for Justice, Truth and Love*. London: Continuum.

Goss, R. E. (1993), *Jesus Acted Up: A Gay and Lesbian Manifesto*. San Francisco: Harper.

Goss, R. E. (1998), 'Sexual Visionaries and Freedom Fighters for a Sexual Reformation: from Gay Theology to Queer Sexual Theologies', in S. Gill (ed.), *The Lesbian and Gay Christian Movement: Campaigning for Justice, Truth and Love*. London: Continuum. pp. 187–202.

Goss, R. E. (1999), 'Queer Theologies as Transgressive Metaphors:

New Paradigms for Hybrid Sexual Theologies'. *Theology and Sexuality* 10, pp. 43–53.

Goss, R. E. (2006), 'John', in D. Guest, R. E. Goss, M. West and T. Bohache (eds), *The Queer Bible Commentary*. London: SCM Press, pp. 548–65.

Graham, E. (2012a), 'Feminist Theory', in B. Miller-McLemore (ed.), *The Wiley-Blackwell Companion to Practical Theology*. London: Blackwell, pp. 193–201.

Graham, E. (2012b), 'A Remembrance of Things (Best) Forgotten: The "Allegorical Past" and the Feminist Imagination'. *Feminist Theology* 21(1), pp. 58–70.

Graham, E. (2012c), 'What's Missing? Gender, Reason and the Post-Secular'. *Political Theology* 13(2), pp. 233–45.

Graham, E. (2013), 'Is Practical Theology a Form of "Action Research"?' *International Journal of Practical Theology* 17(1), pp. 148–78.

Graham, E. with Halsey, M. (1993), *Life-Cycles: Women and Pastoral Care*. London: SPCK.

Graham, R. J. (1989), 'Autobiography and Education'. *Journal of Educational Thought* 23(2), pp. 92–105

Guest, D. (2005), *When Deborah Met Jael*. London: SCM Press.

Guest, D. (2012), *Beyond Feminist Biblical Studies*. Sheffield: Sheffield Phoenix Press.

Halberstam, J. (2011), *The Queer Art of Failure*. Durham, NC: Duke University Press.

Haldeman, D. C. (1994), 'The Practice and Ethics of Sexual Orientation Conversion Therapy'. *Journal of Consulting and Clinical Psychology* 62(2), pp. 221–77.

Hale, C. J. (2003), 'Leatherdyke Boys and Their Daddies: How to Have Sex Without Women or Men', in R. J. Corber and S. Valocchi (eds), *Queer Studies: An Interdisciplinary Reader*. Oxford: Blackwell Publishing, pp. 61–70.

Halperin, D. and Traub, V. (2010), *Gay Shame*. Chicago: Chicago University Press.

Hammers, C. (2014), 'Corporeality, Sadomasochism and Sexual Trauma'. *Body and Society* 20(2), pp. 68–90.

Hardin, K. N. (1999), *The Gay and Lesbian Self-Esteem Book: A Guide to Loving Yourself*. Oakland, CA: New Harbinger Publications.

Hardin, K. N. and Hall, M. (2001), *Queer Blues: The Lesbian and Gay Guide to Overcoming Depression*. Oakland, CA: New Harbinger Publications.

Harrison, M. (2012), 'Non-Directivity, "Being-With" and the Passion of the Christ'. *Thresholds*, Summer 2012, pp. 22–5.

Heckert, J. (2010), 'Intimacy with Strangers/Intimacy with Self: Queer Experiences of Social Research', in K. Browne and C. J. Nash (eds), *Queer Methods and Methodologies*. Ashgate: London, pp. 41–54.

Heelas, P., and Woodhead, L., with Seel, B., Szerszynski, B., and Tusting, K. (2005), *The Spiritual Revolution: Why Religion Is Giving Way to Spirituality*. Oxford: Blackwell.

Heelas, P. (2009), 'Spiritualities of Life', in P. B. Clarke (ed.), *The Oxford Handbook of the Sociology of Religion*. Oxford: Oxford University Press, pp. 758–82.

Herald Scotland (2009), *Obituary, Marcella Althaus-Reid*. Available from http://www.heraldscotland.com/marcella-althaus-reid-1.904743 (accessed 30 April 2016).

Highleyman, L. (1997), 'Playing with Paradox: The Ethics of Erotic Dominance and Submission', in P. Califia and D. Campbell (eds), *Bitch Goddess: The Spiritual Path of the Dominant Woman*. San Francisco: Greenery Press, pp. 153–73.

Hite, S. (1976), *The Hite Report: A Nationwide Study of Female Sexuality*. New York: Seven Stories Press.

Hoeft, J. (2012), 'Gender, Sexism and Heterosexism', in B. Miller-McLemore (ed.), *The Wiley-Blackwell Companion to Practical Theology*. London: Blackwell, pp. 412–21.

Hunt, M. E. (2010), 'Surreal Feminist Liberation Theology: Marcella Althaus-Reid, *Presente!*', in L. Isherwood and M. Jordan (eds), *Dancing Theology in Fetish Boots*. London: Canterbury Press, pp. 17–30.

Isherwood, L. (2003), 'Indecent Theology: What F-ing Difference Does It Make?' *Feminist Theology* 11(2), pp. 141–7.

Isherwood, L. (2010) 'Introduction', in L. Isherwood and M. D. Jordan (eds) (2010), *Dancing Theology in Fetish Boots: Essays in Honour of Marcella Althaus-Reid*. London: SCM Press, pp. xv–xvi.

Isherwood, L. and Stuart, E. (1998), *Introducing Body Theology*. Sheffield: Sheffield Academic Press.

Jagger, A. M. (1989), 'Love and Knowledge'. *Inquiry* 32, pp. 151–76.

Jantzen, G. M. (2001), 'Contours of a Queer Theology'. *Literature and Theology* 13(3), pp. 276–85.

Johnson, E. (1992), *She Who Is: The Mystery of God in Feminist Theological Discourse*. New York: Crossroad.

Johnson, K. (2007), 'Transexualism: Diagnostic Dilemmas, Transgender Politics and the Future of Transgender Care', in V. Clarke and E. Peel (eds), *Out in Psychology: Lesbian, Gay, Bisexual, Trans and Queer Perspectives*. Chichester: John Wiley and Sons, pp. 445–64.

Johnston, L. and Longhurst, R. (2010), *Space, Place and Sex: Geographies of Sexualities*. Lanham: Rowman and Littlefield.

Jordan, M. D. (2000), *The Silence of Sodom: Homosexuality in Modern Catholicism*. Chicago: University of Chicago Press.

Jordan, M. D. (2002), *The Ethics of Sex*. Oxford: Blackwell.

Jung, P. B. (2000), 'Sexual Pleasure: A Roman Catholic Perspective on Women's Delight'. *Theology and Sexuality* 12, pp. 26–47.

Kennedy, P. (2006), *A Modern Introduction to Theology: New Questions for Old Beliefs*. New York: I. B. Tauris.

Kerry, S. C. (2015), 'Intersex and the Role of Religion', in S. Cornwall (ed.), *Intersex, Theology and the Bible: Troubling Bodies in Church, Text and Society*. New York: Palgrave Macmillan, pp. 121–46.

Kessler, K. (2011), 'Showtime Thinks, Therefore I Am: The Corporate Construction of "The Lesbian" on show.com's *The L Word* Site'. *Television and New Media* 14(2), pp. 124–46.

Kitchin, R.M. (1998), 'Towards Geographies of Cyberspace'. *Progress Human Geography* 22, pp. 385–406.

Kinsey, A., Pomeroy, W., Martin, C. and de Cly, E. M. (1948), *Sexual Behavior in the Human Male*, Philadelphia: W.B. Saunders.

Kinsey, A., Pomeroy, W., Martin, C. and Gebhard, P. (1953), *Sexual Behavior in the Human Female*. Philadelphia: W.B. Saunders.

Kocet, M. M., Sanabria, S. and Smith, M. R. (2011), 'Finding the Spirit Within: Religion, Spirituality, and Faith Development in Lesbian, Gay, and Bisexual Individuals', *Journal of LGBT Issues in Counseling* 5(3–4), pp. 163–79.

Kohli, M. (1981), 'Account, Text, Method', in D. Bertaux (ed.),

Biography and Society: The Life History Approach in the Social Sciences. California: Sage, pp. 61–75.

Koosed, J. L. (2006), 'Ecclesiastes/Qohelet', in D. Guest, R. E. Goss, M. West and T. Bohache (eds), *The Queer Bible Commentary.* London: SCM Press, pp. 338–55.

Laccetti, N. (2015), 'Calvary and the Dungeon: Theologizing BDSM', in K. T. Talvacchia, M. F. Pettinger and M. Larrimore (eds)., *Queer Christianities: Lived Religion in Transgressive Forms.* New York: New York University Press, pp. 148–59.

Lake, C. (1999), *Recreations: Religion and Spirituality in the Lives of Queer People.* Toronto: Queer Press.

Lawler, S. (2002), 'Narrative in Social Research', in T. May (ed.), *Qualitative Research in Action.* London: Sage, pp. 242–58.

Lawler, S. (2014), *Identity.* Cambridge: Polity Press.

Lenius, S. (2010), *Life, Leather and the Pursuit of Happiness.* Minneapolis: Nelson Borhek Press.

Levy, D. L. and Reeves, P. (2011), 'Resolving Identity Conflict: Gay, Lesbian, and Queer Individuals with a Christian Upbringing'. *Journal of Gay and Lesbian Social Services,* 23(1), pp. 53–68.

Lindemann, D. (2011), 'BDSM as Therapy?' *Sexualities* 14(2), pp. 151–72

Loughlin, G. (2004), *Alien Sex: The Body and Desire in Cinema and Theology.* Oxford: Blackwell.

Loughlin, G. (2008), 'What is Queer? Theology after Identity'. *Theology and Sexuality* 14(2), pp. 143–52.

Lövheim, M. and Linderman, A. G. (2005), 'Constructing Religious Identity on the Internet', in M. T. Højsgaard and M. Warburg (eds) (2005), *Religion and Cyberspace.* London: Routledge, pp. 121–37.

Lynch, B. (1996), 'Religious and Spiritual Conflicts', in D. Davies and C. Neal (eds), *Pink Therapy: A Guide for Counsellors and Therapists Working with Lesbian, Gay and Bisexual Clients'.* Buckingham: Open University Press, pp. 199–207.

Macke, K. E. (2014), 'Que(e)rying Methodology to Study Church-Based Activism: Conversations in Culture, Power and Change', in Y. Taylor and R. Snowden (eds), *Queering Religion, Religious Queers.* New York: Routledge, pp. 13–30.

Mahoney, A. (2008), 'Is It Possible for Christian Women to Be

Sexual?' *Women and Therapy* 31(1), pp. 89–106.

Mahoney, A. and Espín, O. M. (2008), 'Introduction'. *Women and Therapy* 31(1), pp. 1–4.

Maines, G. (1984), *Urban Aboriginals*. Los Angeles: Daedalus Publishing.

Malinowitz, H. (1993), 'Queer Theory: Whose Theory?' *Frontiers* 13, pp. 168–84.

Mann, R. (2012), *Dazzling Darkness: Gender, Sexuality, Illness and God*. Glasgow: Wild Goose Publications.

McCallum, E. L. and Tuhkanen, M. (eds) (2011), *Queer Times, Queer Becomings*. New York: State University of New York Press.

McCleary, R. (2009), 'Marcella Althaus-Reid: Theology's Bisexual Shock Jock and Queen of Obscene'. Available from http://rollanscensoredissuesblog.blogspot.co.uk/2009/07/marcella-althaus-reid-theologys.html (accessed 30 April 2016).

McClure, B. J. (2008), 'Pastoral Theology as the Art of Paying Attention: Widening the Horizons'. *International Journal of Practical Theology* 12, pp. 189–210.

McGrath, A. E. (1997), *Christian Theology: An Introduction*. Oxford: Blackwell.

McNeill, J. J. (1993), *The Church and the Homosexual*. Boston: Beacon Press.

Mendiger, A. (1983), *Starting an Exodus Ministry Manual*. Baltimore: Regeneration Books.

Mendiger, A. (2000), *Growth into Manhood: Resuming the Journey*. Colorado Springs: Shaw WaterBrook Press.

Merton, R. (1972), 'Insiders and Outsiders: a chapter in the sociology of knowledge'. *American Journal of Sociology* 78, pp. 9–47.

Miller, N. (1991), *Getting Personal: Feminist Occasions and Other Autobiographical Acts*. London: Routledge.

Miller, N. (1995), *Out of the Past: Gay and Lesbian History, From 1869 to the Present*. New York: Vintage Books.

Miller-McLemore, B. J. (1996), 'The Living Human Web: Pastoral Theology at the Turn of the Century', in J. Moessner (ed.), *Through the Eyes of Women: Insights for Pastoral Care*. Minneapolis: Fortress Press, pp. 9–26

Miller-McLemore, B.J. (2012), 'Five Misunderstandings about Practical Theology'. *International Journal of Practical Theology* 16

(1), pp. 5–26.

Miller-McLemore, B. J. and Gill-Austern, B. (eds) (1999), *Feminist and Womanist Pastoral Theology*. Nashville: Abingdon.

Mooney, R. L. (1957), 'The Researcher Himself', in *Research for Curriculum Improvement, Association for Supervision and Curriculum Development, 1957 yearbook*. Washington, DC: Association for Supervision and Curriculum Development, pp. 154–86.

Morland, I. (2009), 'Between Critique and Reform', in M. Homes (ed.), *Critical Intersex*. Farnham: Ashgate, pp. 191–33.

Morton, N. (1986), *The Journey is Home*. Boston, MA: Beacon Press.

Munt, S. (2010), 'Queer Spiritual Spaces', in K. Browne, S. Munt and A. K. T. Yip (eds), *Queer Spiritual Spaces*. Farnham: Ashgate, pp. 1–35.

Namaste, V. (2009), 'Undoing Theory: The "Transgender Question" and the Epistemic Violence of Anglo-American Feminist Theory'. *Hypatia* 24(3), pp. 11–32.

Nelson, J. B. (1979), *Embodiment*. Minneapolis: Augsburg Publishing House.

Nelson, J. B. (1988), *The Intimate Collection*. Philadelphia: The Westminster Press.

Nordling, N., Sandnabba N. K. and Santtila, P. (2000), 'The Prevalence and Effects of Self-Reported Childhood Sexual Abuse Among Sadomasochistically Oriented Males and Females'. *Journal of Child Sexual Abuse* 9(1), pp. 53–63.

Nunkoosing, K. (2005), 'The Problem with Interviews'. *Qualitative Health Research* 15 (5), pp. 698–706.

Nussbaum, M. (1989), 'Narrative Emotions: Beckett's Genealogy of Love', in S. Hauerwas and L. Gregory Jones (eds), *Why Narrative? Readings in Narrative Theology*. Grand Rapids, MI: Eerdmans, pp. 216–48.

O'Riordan, K. and White, H. (2010), 'Virtual Believers: Queer Spiritual Practice Online', in K. Browne, S. Munt and A. k. T. Yip(eds), *Queer Spiritual Spaces*. Farnham: Ashgate, pp. 199–230.

Pattison, S. (2000), *Shame: Theory, Therapy and Theology*. Cambridge: Cambridge University Press.

Pattison, S. (2007), *The Challenge for Practical Theology*. London:

Jessica Kingsley Publishers.

Pears, A. (2004), 'In Context and in Dialogue: Being Indecent with Marcella Althaus-Reid', in A. Pears (ed.), *Feminist Christian Encounters*. Aldershot: Ashgate, pp. 134–62.

Pennebaker J. W. and Seagal J. D. (1999), 'Forming a Story: The Health Benefits of Narrative'. *Journal of Clinical Psychology* 55(10), pp. 1243–54.

Petrella, I. (2010), 'Liberation Theology after Marcella', in L. Isherwood and M. Jordan (eds), *Dancing Theology in Fetish Boots*. London: Canterbury Press, pp. 200–06.

Plummer, K. (1995), *Telling Sexual Stories: Power, Change and Social World*. London: Routledge.

Pui-Lan, K. (2003), 'Theology as a Sexual Act?' *Feminist Theology* 11(2), pp. 149–56.

Pui-Lan, K. (2010), 'Body and Pleasure in Postcoloniality', in L. Isherwood and M. Jordan (eds), *Dancing Theology in Fetish Boots*. London: Canterbury Press, pp. 31–43.

Radford Ruether, R. (1983), *Sexism and God-talk: Toward a Feminist Theology*, Boston: Beacon Press.

Radford Ruether, R. (2010), 'Talking Dirty, Speaking Truth: Indecenting Theology', in L. Isherwood and M. Jordan (eds), *Dancing Theology in Fetish Boots*. London: Canterbury Press, pp. 254–67.

Ratzinger, J. (2004), 'Europe: Its Spiritual Foundation: Yesterday, Today and in the Future'. Available from https://www.catholicculture.org/culture/library/view.cfm?recnum=6317 (accessed 30 April 2016).

Reason, P. and Hawkins, P., (1988), 'Storytelling as Inquiry', in P. Reason (ed.), *Human Inquiry in Action: Developments in New Paradigm Research*. London: SAGE, pp. 79–101.

Rich, A. (1980), 'Toward a Woman-Centred University', in A. Rich (ed.), *On Lies, Secrets and Silence: Selected Prose 1966–78*. New York: W.W. Norton and Co., pp. 23–75.

Ricoeur, P. (1980), 'Narrative and Time'. *Critical Inquiry* 7(1), pp. 160–90.

Rivera Rivera, M. (2010), 'Corporeal Visions and Apparitions: The Narrative Strategies of an Indecent Theologian', in Isherwood, L. and Jordan, M. (eds), *Dancing Theology in Fetish Boots*. London:

Canterbury Press, pp. 79–94.

Rix, J. (2010), *Ex-gay, No Way: Survival and Recovery from Religious Abuse*. Forres: Findhorn Press.

Robinson, M. (2010), 'Reading Althaus-Reid: As a Bi Feminist Theo/Methodological Resource'. *Journal of Bisexuality* 10, pp. 108–20.

Roman Catholic Church (1992), *Catechism of the Catholic Church*. Available from http://www.vatican.va/archive/ccc_css/archive/catechism/p3s2c2a6.htm (accessed 30 April 2016).

Rowan, J. (2005), 'The Humanistic Approach to Action Research', in P. Reason and H. Bradbury (eds), *Handbook of Action Research*. London: Sage, pp. 106–16.

Rubin, G. (1984), 'Thinking Sex: Notes for a Radical Theory of the Politics of Sexuality', in H. Abelove, M. A. Barale and D. Halperin (eds), *The Lesbian and Gay Studies Reader*. London: Routledge, 1993, pp. 3–44.

Rubin, G. (2009), 'A Little Humility', in D. Halperin and V. Traub (eds), *Gay Shame*. Chicago: University of Chicago Press, pp. 369–73.

Rules from the Love in Action Program (no date), Available from http://www.boxturtlebulletin.com/Articles/000,022.htm (accessed 30 April 2016).

Sands, K. M. (2010), 'Civil Unions, Colonialism and the Struggle for Sexual Decency in Hawaii', in L. Isherwood and M. Jordan (eds), *Dancing Theology in Fetish Boots*. London: Canterbury Press, pp. 44–60.

Sassen, S. (2002), 'Towards a Sociology of Information Technology'. *Current Sociology* 50(3), pp. 365–88.

Schuck, K. D. and Liddle, B. J. (2001), 'Religious Conflicts Experienced by Lesbian, Gay, and Bisexual Individuals'. *Journal of Gay and Lesbian Psychotherapy* 5(2), pp. 63–82.

Scott, J. W. (1991), 'The Evidence of Experience'. *Critical Inquiry* 17 (4), pp. 773–97.

Segundo, J. L. (1988), *An Evolutionary Approach to Jesus of Nazareth*. Edited and translated by John Drury. New York: Orbis Books.

Sharma, S. (2011), *Good Girls, Good Sex: Women Talk about Church and Sexuality*. Halifax, NS: Fernwood Publishing.

Shore-Goss, R. E. (2010), 'Dis/Grace-full Incarnation and the Dis/Grace-full Church: Marcella Althaus-Reid's Vision of Radical Inclusivity', in L. Isherwood and M. Jordan (eds), *Dancing Theology in Fetish Boots*. London: Canterbury Press, pp. 1–16.

Simpson, R. H. (2005), 'How to Be Fashionably Queer: Reminding the Church of the Importance of Sexual Stories'. *Theology and Sexuality* 11(2), pp. 97–108.

Simula, B. L. (2013), 'Queer Utopias in Painful Spaces: BDSM Participants' Interrelational Resistance to Heteronormativity and Gender Regulation', in A. Jones (ed.), *A Critical Inquiry into Queer Utopias*. New York: Palgrave MacMillan, pp. 71–100.

Slevin, J. (2000), *The Internet and Society*. Cambridge: Polity Press.

Sloan, L. J. (2015), 'Ace of (BDSM), Clubs: Building Asexual Relationships through BDSM Practice'. *Sexualities* 18(5–6), pp. 548–63.

Spelman, E.V. (1988), *Inessential Woman: Problems of Exclusion in Feminist Thought*. Boston: Beacon Press.

Stanley, L. (1992), *The Auto/biographical I*. Manchester: Manchester University Press.

Stern, S. R. (2003), 'Encountering Distressing Information in Online Research: A Consideration of Legal and Ethical Responsibilities'. *New Media Society* 5, pp. 249–66.

Stone, H. W. and Duke, J. O. (2006), *How to Think Theologically*. Minneapolis: Fortress Press.

Stone, K. (2007), 'Gender Criticism: The Un-Manning of Abimelech', in G. A. Yee (ed.), *Judges and Method: New Approaches in Biblical Studies*. Minneapolis: Fortress Press, pp. 183–201.

Stringer, M. D. (1997), 'Expanding the Boundaries of Sex: An Exploration of Sexual Ethics After the Second Sexual Revolution', *Theology and Sexuality* 4(7), pp. 27–43.

Stuart, E. (1995), *Just Good Friends: Towards a Lesbian and Gay Theology of Relationships*. London: Mowbrays.

Stuart, E. (1997a), *Religion is a Queer Thing*. London: Cassell.

Stuart, E. (1997b) 'Sex in Heaven: The Queering of Theological Discourse on Sexuality', in J. Davies and G. Loughlin (eds). *Sex These Days. Essay on Theology, Sexuality and Society*. Sheffield: Sheffield Academic Press. pp.184–204.

Stuart, E. (2003), *Gay and Lesbian Theologies: Repetitions and Critical Difference*. Aldershot: Ashgate.

Stuart, E. (2007), 'Sacramental Flesh', in G. Loughlin (ed.), *Queer Theology: Rethinking the Western Body*. London: Blackwell, pp. 65–75.

Stuart, E. (2010), 'Making No Sense: Liturgy as a Queer Space', in L. Isherwood and M. Jordan (eds), *Dancing Theology in Fetish Boots*. London: Canterbury Press, pp. 113–23.

Stuart, E. (2014), 'The Theological Study of Sexuality', in A. Thatcher (ed.), *The Oxford Handbook of Theology, Sexuality and Gender*. Oxford: Oxford University Press, pp. 18–31.

Sweasey, P. (1997), *From Queer to Eternity*. London: Cassell.

Talvacchia, K. T. (2015), 'Disrupting the Theory-Practice Binary', in K. T. Talvacchia, M. F. Pettinger and M. Larrimore (eds), *Queer Christianities: Lived Religion in Transgressive Forms*. New York: New York University Press, pp. 184–94.

Taylor, G. W. and Ussher, J. M. (2001), 'Making Sense of S&M: A Discourse Analytic Account'. *Sexualities* 4(3), pp. 293–314.

This Is What Love in Action Looks Like (2011) (DVD), Morgan Jon Fox, USA. Available: TLA Releasing.

Thomas, C. (2000), *Straight with a Twist*. Chicago: University of Illinois Press.

Tigert, L. (1999), *Coming Out Through Fire*. Eugene, OR: Pilgrim Press.

Turkle, S. (1995), *Life on the Screen*. New York: Simon and Schuster.

Van der Kolk, B. A. (1996), 'The Black Hole of Trauma', in B. A. Van der Kolk, A. C. McFarlane and L. Weisaeth (eds), *Traumatic Stress: The Effects of Overwhelming Experience on Mind, Body and Society*. New York: Guildford Press, pp. 5–23.

Waites, M. (2005), *The Age of Consent: Young People, Sexuality and Citizenship*. London: Palgrave Macmillan.

Ward, G. (2010), 'Queer Theory, Hermeneutics and the Limits of Libertinism', in L. Isherwood and M. Jordan (eds), *Dancing Theology in Fetish Boots*. London: Canterbury Press, pp. 166–80.

Warner, M. (1993), *Fear of a Queer Planet*. Minneapolis: University of Minnesota Press.

Warner, D. N. (2004), 'Towards a Queer Research Methodology'.

Qualitative Research in Psychology 1(4), pp. 321–37.

Winterson, J. (1995), *Art Objects: Essays on Ecstasy and Effrontery.* London: Vintage Books.

Wittig, M. (1994), *The Straight Mind and Other Essays.* Boston: Beacon Press.

Wolkomir, M. (2001), 'Wrestling with the Angels of Meaning: The Revisionist Ideological Work of Gay and Ex-Gay Men'. *Symbolic Interaction* 24, pp. 407–24.

Wolkomir, M. (2006), *Be Not Deceived: The Sacred and Sexual Struggles of Gay and Ex-Gay Christian Men.* New Brunswick, NJ: Rutgers University Press.

Woodhead, L. (1997), 'Sex in a Wider Context', in J. Davies and G. Loughlin (eds), *Sex These Days.* Sheffield: Sheffield Academic Press, pp. 98–121.

Woodhead, L. *Religion and Public Life* and *Religion and Personal Life* research projects. Available from http://faithdebates.org.uk/research/ (accessed 30 April 2016),

Woodward, T. (1998), 'Editorial', *Skin Two* 27 (Autumn), p. 7.

Yip, A. K. T. (1997a), *Gay Male Christian Couples.* London: Praeger.

Yip, A. K. T. (1997b), 'Gay Male Couples and Sexual Exclusivity'. *Sociology* 31, pp. 289–306.

Yip, A. K. T. (1998), 'Gay Male Christians' Perceptions of the Christian Community in Relation to their Sexuality'. *Theology and Sexuality* 8, pp. 40–51.

Yip, A. K. T. (2000), 'Leaving the Church to Keep My Faith: The Lived Experiences of Non-heterosexual Christians', in L. J. Francis and Y. J. Katz (eds), *Joining and Leaving Religion: Research Perspectives.* Leominster: Gracewing, pp. 129–45.

Yip, A. K. T (2002), 'The Persistence of Faith Among Nonheterosexual Christians: Evidence for the Neosecularization Book of Religious Transformation'. *Journal for the Scientific Study of Religion* 41(2), pp. 199–212.

Yip, A. K. T. (2003a), 'Spirituality and Sexuality: An Exploration of the Religious Beliefs of Non-Heterosexual Christians in Great Britain'. *Theology and Sexuality* 9(2), pp. 137–54.

Yip, A. K. T. (2003b), 'Sexuality and the Church'. *Sexualities* 6(1), pp. 60–4.

REFERENCES

Yip, A. K. T. (2003c), 'The Self as the Basis of Religious Faith: Spirituality of Gay, Lesbian and Bisexual Christians', in G. Davie, P. Heelas and L. Woodhead (eds), *Predicting Religion: Christian, Secular and Alternative Futures*. Aldershot: Ashgate, pp. 135–46.

Yip, A. K. T (2005), 'Queering Religious Texts: An Exploration of British Non-heterosexual Christians' and Muslims' Strategy of Constructing Sexuality-affirming Hermeneutics'. *Sociology* 39, pp. 47–65.

Yip, A. K. T. (2010a), 'Coming Home from the Wilderness: An Overview of Recent Scholarly Research on LGBTQI Religiosity/Spirituality', in K. Browne, S. R. Munt and A. K. T. Yip (eds), *Queer Spiritual Spaces: Sexuality and Sacred Places*. Farnham: Ashgate, pp. 35–50.

Yip, A. K. T. (2010b), 'Special Feature: Sexuality and Religion/Spirituality'. *Sexualities* 13(6), pp. 667–70.

Zussman, M. (2001), 'Fairy Butch and the Labia Menorah: A Queer Example of Ludic Parody, Play and Performance Art'. *European Journal of Anthropology* 37, pp. 77–88.

Zussman, M. and Pierce, A. (1988), 'Shifts of Consciousness in Consensual S/M, Bondage and Fetish Play', *Anthropology of Consciousness* 9(4), pp. 15–38.

Notes

1 Examples of stories based on biographical and experiential explorations include Crew, 1991; Sweasey, 1997; Lake, 1999; Ford, 2004; Yip, 2000; 2002; 2003a; 2003b; 2010b.

2 For example, Graham, 1993; 2012a; 2012b; 2012c; Miller-McLemore and Gill-Austern, 1999; Miller-McLemore, 2012.

3 See Radford Ruether, 1983; Daly, 1985; Johnson, 1992; Coakley, 2003; Bacon, 2009 for examples.

4 See, for instance, Fortunato, 1982; Clark, 1989; 1997; Comstock, 1993; 1996; McNeill, 1993.

5 See, for example, Hardin, 1999; Hardin and Hall, 2001; Halperin and Traub, 2010.

6 See Culbertson and Krondorfer (2005) for further discussion on men's studies in religion.

7 A 'violet wand' is a stimulation toy which applies an electrical impulse to the body as part of sensual play.

8 A 'pin wheel' or 'Wartenberg pinwheel' is a tool consisting of sharp pins which are rotated across the recipient's flesh.

9 'Shibari' is a form of Japanese rope bondage, in which the rope not only serves to restrain an individual, but it is done so to present the rope itself in an artistic form.

10 See also Joseph Bean (2001) for further examples of the spiritual element of BDSM practice. Similarly, Geoff Maines's work

on the spiritual dimension of leather sexuality (1984).

11 In highlighting the long history of erotophobia within Christianity in particular, we observe a deep ambivalence within positional statements about the function and role of sexual relations. In the Church of England's *Issues in Human Sexuality* there is this extract: 'In all ages some have seen in sexual ecstasy an entry into the realm of the divine, or have made sexual activity a ritual for securing divine blessing on human life. The Judaeo-Christian tradition has ... been implacably opposed to this divinisation of sex. Although erotic imagery has been one appropriate way of describing mystical union through prayer, there has also in Christian spirituality been a cautiousness about erotic pleasure. Because "being in love" is all pervasive, driving other concerns to the margins of attention, and because love-making is an authentically ecstatic experience, excluding everything else from consciousness, the Church has tended to see sexual attraction and activity as particularly hostile to God's due place as the supreme object of human love and the proper controller of all human thought, feeling and conduct.' The report goes on to state: 'western society today has become widely obsessed with sexual pleasure as an end in itself' (1991, pp. 27–8). See also, Isherwood and Stuart (1998), ch. 3, 'A Difficult Relationship: Christianity and the Body'.

12 See, for example, the data collated by Linda Woodhead in the *Religion and Public Life* and *Religion and Personal Life* research projects. Available from http://faithdebates.org.uk/research/ (accessed 30 April 2016).

Index of Names and Subjects

INDEX

INDEX

INDEX

INDEX

INDEX

INDEX

INDEX

INDEX

INDEX

INDEX

Fear of Queer Planet, 11–12
White, Heather, 78–9
The Windsor Report (Anglican Communion), 103
Winquist, Charles, 42
Winterson, Jeannette, 184
Wolkomir, Michelle
  emotions of ex-gays, 109, 110
  ex-gay belonging, 111, 112, 115–17
Woodhead, Linda
  on Nelson, 8
  subjective over institutional, 27
Woodward, T., 141

Yip, Andrew K. T., 7
  Althaus-Reid and, 36
  ethnography of LBG Christians, 162–3, 164
  Gay Male Christian Couples, 36
  non-academic storytelling, 27
  sexuality and religion, 34–6

Zussman, Mira
  BDSM as ecstatic religion, 157
  BDSM as therapy, 143
  'Fairy Butch and the Labia Menorah,' 152
  performative gender, 148
  SM transcendence, 142
  trust of bondage, 139